Introductory note

This collection is a political byproduct of the editorial work to prepare issue no. 11 of *New International* magazine, which features the resolution adopted by the 1990 convention of the Socialist Workers Party, "U.S. Imperialism Has Lost the Cold War." In the course of that work, the editors noticed that several reports or letters referred to in that resolution were no longer easily available in print. What's more, those reports remain part of the foundation of the SWP's turn to the industrial unions and proletarian political course that are central not only to the 1990 document but also to the reports and resolutions collected in *The Changing Face of U.S. Politics: Working-Class Politics and the Trade Unions* by SWP national secretary Jack Barnes (Pathfinder: 1981, 2002 [2011 printing]).

At a time when labor resistance to employer assaults on workers' living standards and union rights is accelerating more than at any time since 1989–90—and when opportunities for mass work are expanding for members of the Socialist Workers Party and Young Socialists in the United States, as well as for communist workers and youth in other countries—the publication of these reports seems not only timely but obligatory.

This Education for Socialists booklet is published in that spirit, with confidence that readers will find it a useful companion to *The Changing Face of U.S. Politics* and "U.S. Imperialism Has Lost the Cold War," as well as to other books, pamphlets, and issues of *New International* distributed by Pathfinder.

Steve Clark
SEPTEMBER 4, 1998

BUILDING THE PARTY'S NINE NATIONAL INDUSTRIAL UNION FRACTIONS

By Joel Britton

The following report was adopted by the Thirty-third Constitutional Convention of the Socialist Workers Party in August 1985.

The purpose of this report is not to discuss implementation of our fall tasks and perspectives by the industrial union fractions around the South Africa and Central America campaigns, the fight for women's rights, the Black struggle, circulation of our press, and so on. Nor is the purpose to discuss the interrelationship of branch and fraction work in carrying out these tasks. That has been done at the meetings of each of our nine national union fractions earlier this week, as well as at the other fraction meetings and workshops that have been held here during the convention.

This report will also not reexamine the current stage of the employers' antilabor offensive and their rout of the AFL-CIO officialdom. Events of the last few months have confirmed our views on this, and the preconvention discussion indicated broad agreement in the party on the evaluation adopted by the National Committee at its May meeting.

Instead, our aim here is to summarize the conclusions of a report by Mac Warren that was adopted by the July meeting of the National Committee, and to draw on the experience and thinking of the delegates on these matters related to strengthening our nine national industrial union fractions. Today's report assumes the political framework of the resolution that is before the convention for a vote: "Revolutionary Perspective and Leninist Continuity in the United States" [see issue no. 4 of *New International*]. It builds on the trade-union reports adopted at the May NC meeting, as well as the two reports adopted by the Political Committee concerning the June meeting of SWP members in the United Auto Workers union. The motion to approve the general line of the political resolution incorporates the general line of these three trade-union reports, and any discussion on them is in order.

The meetings of the nine national fractions that have taken place here not only showed that we still have a lot of work ahead of us in building and rebuilding our fractions—which we already knew—but also registered some solid progress by the party over the past period in doing this.

National fractions

First, the party has more genuinely *national* industrial union fractions today. In the case of several fractions, this is true for the first time since we began building them.

Our fractions need to be genuinely national, not only because we are building a nationwide party, but also because the unions we belong to are national (and in some cases include a Canadian component, as well). That is, these unions are spread geographically across the United States like the industries they organize.

Our participation in them as union builders, as revolutionary union politicians, is more effective—and can only be effective—as we gain varied experience in workplaces and locals across the country, not in just a few cities. There is no such thing as a "typical" local of an industrial union. By having party members from *more of our branches* represented in each one of the nine national fractions, we draw on the experience of a broader layer of the union membership of our class, and of our own cadres. We find out how ignorant a small organization such as ours really is about the industrial union movement in this country. And we begin to expand our knowledge and spread it throughout the party.

That is why it's so important, for example, to maintain and strengthen the party branches that are key to building United Mine Workers fractions in the coalfields of West Virginia, Pennsylvania, southern Illinois, Alabama, and in a center of western mining—Price, Utah. We are learning more and more about the mining industry and about the UMW, the challenges before it, and the past struggles that bear on these challenges. As developments such as the Coal Employment Project have occurred—endorsed by the union, and reflecting the aspirations of a layer of women miners from Appalachia to Illinois, from Alabama to the Navajo Nation—our UMW fractions have found themselves right where the action is in quite a few parts of the country.

Branching out in our unions

In order to build genuinely national fractions, we have also learned that we need to branch out from the sector of production that the union is predominantly based in, or may have originated in, into other *related* sectors of production. Our experience has demonstrated that too narrowly defining the "key sectors" organized by a union can be misleading in constructing our national fractions.

For instance, as we've learned more about the United Steelworkers and United Auto Workers unions, we have understood the need to build USWA and UAW fractions in plants beyond basic steel and auto assembly. We're paying more attention to building fractions in steel fabricating shops and auto parts plants, in USWA-organized oil-tool factories and UAW-organized aerospace plants. As a result, we're getting to know workers in these unions whose wages and conditions are different from what we've seen before. We're becoming part of the workforce in other sectors of these industries and unions, and have found that the employer offensive takes some different forms, and has different paces in each of them. We've also discovered that the response of the workers and their political experiences are often different.

Over the past several years, the layoffs and plant shutdowns in basic steel and auto assembly forced us to take jobs wherever we could find them in order to maintain a presence in these unions. We often had little or no control over the matter.

For the time being, we still remain out of basic steel. We are in contact with that sector of the union through our national and local USWA fractions, however, and we are on the lookout in a number of branches for opportunities to get back in.

The upturn in auto production in the recent period, on the other hand, presented us both with some opportunities and some new, and not totally anticipated, challenges. I'll come back to this.

Our national fraction in the International Association of Machinists decided at its meeting a year ago to build fractions in IAM-organized airlines, in addition to the aerospace and war plants where we had previously been centered. Four party branches now have fractions at airports. This has made it possible for the IAM fraction to develop a geographic spread among a wider layer of branches than ever before and to get a more accurate understanding of that union.

Having these local IAM fractions has also brought us into closer contact with workers who are bearing the brunt of the sharp drive by the owners of the airlines to slash wages and impose other takebacks. We've been in a better position to relate to the strike struggles at United and Pan Am over the past year, as well as to contract battles by workers at other airlines.

At its national fraction meeting here a few days ago, the Oil, Chemical and Atomic Workers fraction decided to encourage branches to build fractions in the chemical industry. Up to now, our national OCAW fraction has been centered in the union's oil refinery division. As we've gotten to know the union better, we've recently learned that about half of the union membership is in its chemical division. A good number of the local and district officials leading the fight to prevent OCAW from being weakened by a proposed merger with the United Paperworkers International Union, are in the chemical division. By encouraging branches to start looking for opportunities to build local fractions in the refinery *and* the chemical divisions, we'll both strengthen the nationwide character of the national OCAW fraction and develop a better knowledge of the union as a whole.

The same basic considerations hold true for all nine national fractions, although we face different concrete choices in each of them. Expanding our focus to more than one industrial sector of these unions will enable more branches to build fractions in them, and thus allow for stronger and more genuinely national fractions.

All nine fractions

Our discussions in the fraction meetings here have confirmed that the party can carry out our political perspectives in all nine industrial unions where we have decided to build national fractions.

Of course, we discover a wide variety of practices and traditions from one union to the other. The composition of the workforce differs in each of them. Wage and benefit levels are different, as well as working conditions. There are variations among them in how the employer offensive is being conducted, and in the current level of response by the membership. And within each of the nine unions, situations vary widely from local to local, as well.

In all nine of these unions the officials are not only class-collaborationist but are open advocates of capitalism; all are bureaucratic. But the breed of misleadership differs from one to the other. Although the officialdom is not qualitatively better or worse in any one of them, the differences sometimes are big enough to make it a bit harder or a bit easier for us and other unionists to function, especially on the local and district level.

In none of these nine industrial unions, however, is there any motion whatsoever today toward the development of a class-struggle left wing. While the employers' offensive has intensified and class polarization has deepened over the past decade, finance capital remains on the offensive. There has been resistance in the working class, of course. We have participated in some of these fights, as well as helped build labor solidarity with the workers and unions in struggle. We are part of the discussion among growing numbers of workers about why the unions aren't beating back the employers' blows, and how to begin to defend ourselves more effectively. But setbacks continue to outpace advances, and labor remains on the defensive.

A break from the officialdom's class-collaborationist subordination of the unions to capitalist profit needs can only emerge out of struggles by an aroused and combative rank and file. And it will take form around a political program that offers a class-struggle alternative to the course being charted by the current misleaders of the labor movement. As that begins to happen in sections of the labor movement, the fight to forge a class-struggle left wing will be posed in practice. And that's still down the road a ways.

Not a matter of will power

So, we need to learn to relax and not get frustrated about the current pace of events. *We can't move the class, we have to move with the class.* That's the beginning of wisdom for all nine of our union fractions.

There's a lot that every one of our fractions can do in each of the nine unions. But the one thing that we can't do in any of them is *will* the struggle onward. There is not some opportunity in any of these nine unions right now that would lead us to take special priority measures in order to be part of some development that is substantially changing the U.S. labor movement. From our standpoint as a party of worker-bolsheviks, building each of the nine industrial union fractions is equally important politically.

None of these unions even has a serious reform movement today that seeks to mobilize the ranks for more militant struggle against the employers and for greater union democracy. In the late 1960s and in the 1970s there were two, and only two, such developments—the Miners for Democracy movement in the UMW, and Steelworkers Fightback in the USWA.

This doesn't mean that there aren't some important differences in the internal life and extent of rank-and-file involvement among these nine industrial unions.

The clearest example is the UMW. In the late sixties and early seventies, the Miners for Democracy movement took on the coal operators and the government—basically combining the fight around safety and around black lung benefits. It swept the corrupt and bureaucratic Boyle officialdom out of its way in the course of that fight for control over and improvements in health and safety conditions. The Miners for Democracy conquered a degree of greater control over the UMW by the ranks that has enabled them to more effectively wield union power against the bosses ever since. That was demonstrated in the strike battles of 1978 and 1981, and even today the coal operators have not yet been able to impose the kind of takeback contract that has become the norm in other industries. This is true despite the progress that the UMW officialdom has subsequently made in eroding some of the past gains in democratic functioning, thereby weakening the union.

The development of the Coal Employment Project in the UMW is another development that has no parallel in other unions right now. The CEP gives our UMW fraction some special opportunities.

These factors are important for our fraction-building work in the UMW. They underline the importance of recent moves we have made to reinforce our branches in coal-mining areas, as we move toward making more of them multifraction branches and stronger political units of the party. These are not the kind of developments, however, that would cause us to give the UMW some special priority today over the other eight unions in our overall fraction orientation.

We're trying to build all nine.

Multifraction branches

What forced us to think out these questions most clearly was the mushrooming size of our United Auto Workers fraction. Over the past year hiring opened up in the big auto assembly plants once again. In a number of branches, however, a flood into auto developed, without sufficient consideration to the party's overall fraction-building perspectives and the negative political consequences of having almost all working members in a single large fraction. Local fractions in other of the nine priority unions were dissolved, without thinking out the implications of doing so. This was especially true of fractions in the International Ladies' Garment Workers' Union and the Amalgamated Clothing and Textile Workers Union, but also in the USWA and OCAW. Folding up these local fractions left our branches weaker politically in a number of cities, and weakened our union work as a whole in the party.

As a result of this rush into auto, by the beginning of this summer the UAW fraction comprised fully one-fourth of the number of party members that we had in the nine national fractions altogether.

There was no political development in the UAW that could justify this big tide away from other fractions into auto. In fact, in some cases—including in building support for the April 20 antiwar and anti-apartheid actions—our local UAW fractions had more difficulty getting official backing than our fractions in other of the nine unions. We got at least as much, and often more, official endorsement and active participation in the ILGWU, ACTWU, the USWA, the United Transportation Union, the IAM, OCAW, and the International Union of Electronic Workers.

We've drawn some lessons from these experiences.

The more of the nine fractions a branch is building, the stronger it will be politically, and the better feel it will have for what's going on in the labor movement and in the politics of its area. It will be in touch with the problems and possibilities among a cross section of the working class and the unions. Multifraction branches carry out better and more energetic election campaigns—not geared so much to one or two industries and unions, but directed to the broader working-class public and labor movement, and oriented around our overall political program.

The party has had some other experiences with one-fraction branches over the years, and the outcome has been politically disastrous. In 1948 the Indiana Harbor "steel branch" was entirely oriented to building a USWA fraction; it lost its political bearings around the liberal capitalist Progressive Party presidential campaign, and we ended up losing the whole unit (as well as much of our national USWA fraction). A few years later, the Cochran faction had its stronghold in what was for all intents and purposes the one-fraction "UAW branch" in Detroit.

We can sometimes get the misimpression that Minneapolis was a one-fraction "Teamster branch" in the 1930s. But it never was, and was consciously built *not* to be. The comrades in Local 574 (and later 544), of course, were an important component of the branch membership and leadership. But there were always comrades in other industries and union fractions. This helped the branch set an example for the whole party as a well-rounded *political* unit of worker-bolsheviks doing socialist propaganda work throughout the city and around the state. And there was never a less provincial nor more internationalist branch in the SWP.

Oversized fractions

Pouring so many comrades into big auto assembly plants over the past year also posed the question of fraction size and functioning in a new and sharper way for the entire party. We talked this out at the July National Committee meeting and at all the fraction meetings here this week.

The curse of oversized fractions has become a problem in more and more branches. Through assessing our experience, we've come to the conclusion that fractions of 2, 3, or 4 comrades are much more effective for the type of work we can and should be doing as revolutionary politicians in the unions. (Of course, we're not talking here about fractions that grow big through recruitment of workers to the party. We look forward to the day when *that* begins to happen in a lot of our branches.)

What is an oversized fraction?

One where we begin to feel that the party will attract more support and adherents because of our numbers in the plant or union local. That we will get a lot more accomplished that way.

One where we begin to get remarks or questions from coworkers—even from friendly co-workers—asking us why so many socialists seem to be auto workers, or oil workers, or IAM members. Where a co-worker comes to his or her first party event and already knows most of the branch members. We've gotten into these kinds of situations with co-workers at the Budd auto parts plant in Philadelphia, where we had eight or nine members; at the big FMC tank plant in San Jose, where we've had fifteen to twenty; and at the Chevron oil refinery in the Bay Area, where we're now up to nine.

An oversized fraction is one where we can hardly help developing notions of "power." Where we begin to exaggerate our immediate influence in the union, to misread the real relationship of forces.

Until the rude awakening.

An instructive example was presented by a comrade at the USWA fraction meeting. We had a local fraction of eleven in the USWA local that includes the Sloan Valve Plant in Chicago, where most of the fraction works. Most of the union meetings are small, as union meetings usually are in this period. We never had all eleven comrades attend, but, even so, we could still get things adopted and seemed to be a force at local meetings.

Until the rude awakening.

The fraction decided that it was going to propose at one union meeting that a Coalition of Labor Union Women representative come to an upcoming meeting to report on the CLUW convention. The officials knew and liked the CLUW representative, so we thought it would be a cinch. Totally legitimate. Who could object?

But the local officials and their people voted it down. After the meeting, one of the officials came up to a leader of the fraction and said something to this effect: "That was just so your caucus knows what the score is around here."

So, as one rule of thumb, we should know that we've got an oversized fraction when we have to go month after month deciding *not* to have fraction members go to their union meeting, because we don't want to have too imposing a presence.

An oversized fraction is more.

It's when we begin relying on fraction members to get things done in and around the union, instead of our main work being to involve co-workers in whatever way possible. When it begins to seem easier just to do it ourselves, rather than to reach out to union brothers and sisters, who, with a little motivation and encouragement, will take on more responsibility.

We're in an oversized fraction when we spend more time organizing ourselves than organizing and talking to other workers and union activists. We're almost always doing something wrong when we end up making a union leaflet for the April 20 bus ourselves, rather than getting a co-worker involved along with us. We should be looking for any chance to have a co-worker be the union's representative to an April 20 coalition, instead of a member of our fraction, even though we may have taken the initiative in raising the issue in our union. We want our union sisters and brothers to chair the local's program on sexual harassment, the slide show on apartheid or on Nicaragua, and so on. That's our goal.

We're an oversized fraction when each of us

doesn't worry much about whether or not something that the fraction decided to do will actually get done, since comrade A, B, C, D, E, or F "is taking care of it," or "has more experience than I do at that kind of thing, anyway." When we're not challenging every member of the fraction to contribute all she or he is capable of in carrying out our work in the union.

When we get locked into the mode of functioning of an oversized fraction, it's harder to turn outward, to shed vestiges of our semisectarian existence. It becomes easy both to underutilize the political capacities of each and every comrade in the fraction, while at the same time isolating ourselves from new and living forces and struggles in our unions and in the broader labor movement.

The branch leadership ends up not paying attention to some of the smaller fractions, or to comrades working by themselves in a union situation, since it's spending so much time working with the one big fraction in the branch.

All of these results of oversized fractions reinforce the political narrowness that develops in a one- or two-fraction branch. And stripping down the size of an oversized fraction is often the only way we can begin to make progress in building fractions in some other of the nine priority unions.

'One-person fractions'

We sometimes have opportunities to get a comrade hired into a job in one of the nine unions we've been trying to get into, but under conditions where he or she is going to have to function for a while as the only party member in that workplace. That's not our goal, of course; we're always aiming to get one or two more feet in the door. But that can take some time.

We need to pay attention to these comrades, who are a bit more on their own in functioning politically on the job and in the union. A comrade working such a job is not part of a branch fraction (unless there are other branch members in the same union working at another plant). But he or she *is* a member of one of the nine national fractions.

Where we're in that situation—waiting for a reinforcement or two, or a recruit or two, or for a chance to move into a place where we do have a fraction—we should think of ourselves as sort of a fraction of one. We're not really part of a fraction in the sense of an organized group of two or more comrades, of course. But that doesn't mean that we can't do many of the things that a fraction does. A comrade can be very effective in such a situation, especially if she or he doesn't come under pressure to do more than one person can do.

Branch leaderships shouldn't look at comrades in such jobs as if they're just marking time and making a living until some other comrade gets in, or until they get another job as part of a fraction. *We should work with these comrades and help them carry out political work in their unions.* Often these "one-person fractions" can be more effective than an oversized fraction.

What about the need felt by some comrades for the personal and political reinforcement that they feel they get from being part of a bigger fraction?

At the OCAW fraction meeting a couple of days ago, a party member from Toledo related an experience that she had not too long ago at a refinery where she is the only comrade. She had come under a lot of pressure on the job as the result of some sexist harassment. This harassment was company-inspired, but, as is often the case, involved some co-workers who needed to be educated in working-class solidarity and common decency. Since this comrade wasn't part of a fraction there, she had no choice but to seek out some co-workers. And she got the help that she needed in dealing with the situation.

Of course, any comrade—female or male—who is facing harassment on the job should approach it as a party problem, not a personal one. If there is no fraction, then he or she should raise it directly with the branch executive committee, and should get whatever collective help is needed to deal with the problem in a timely fashion.

Whether or not we have a fraction, however, the key to dealing with such situations is reaching out to others in the union and on the job who can help raise the matter in the union and bring pressure on the boss.

It's a myth that these kinds of day-to-day problems of individual party members get more attention in very large fractions. In fact, they often get shunted aside or not dealt with in a timely way. There just seems to be too many people in the fraction to set aside time to discuss each member's situation. Instead, we can end up exhorting each other to do all the things we have agreed on. We don't take the time to discuss how we're going to collectively carry out the work; how to handle any problems individual comrades are bumping up against; and how we're going to draw co-workers into activity and around the party and Young Socialist Alliance.

Our one UTU member in the Bay Area couldn't depend on any direct reinforcement from other party members in building the April 20 demonstration in the rail yards, since there hasn't been any hiring. So, she talked it over with her co-workers and with some local UTU officials, and they worked together to build a contingent of UTU members with official union backing. She got some important help from the Bay Area trade-union leadership. Bay Area comrades I've talked to judge that the work of this one-person semi-fraction was more effective in building April 20 through the unions than the work of our oversized fractions out there.

A bias toward propagandism

Building smaller fractions and multifraction branches also creates the best conditions for us to carry out more rounded political work in the unions, as effective revolutionary politicians and bold communist workers. A bias in the direction of propagandism begins to develop when we have the notion that we've got to pour into the auto assembly plants while there's hiring, but that it's just a matter of time before we're all laid off again.

That approach, in fact, was gaining some ground in the party, especially following the 1981–82 recession. We were beginning to develop a "boom and bust" approach to fraction-building in some cases. Rather than looking toward developing long-term, stable fraction work in the unions, we were sometimes tempted by the rationalization that we had better make a big political splash in the union while we had the chance, since it was likely that our fraction could be wiped out again at any moment.

One result was a one-sided emphasis on moving around our press, our books, and our socialist election material as virtually the be-all and end-all of fraction activity. As important and indispensable as this is to any real communist work in the unions, it is not a substitute for doing what the political resolution calls "striv[ing] to develop the ability to function as effective units that are integrated into the labor movement," and "function[ing] collectively as union politicians." There was a bias toward functioning in the unions almost solely on the first of the three levels outlined for our union fractions in the political resolution—toward wearing only one of the "three hats." [See section entitled "Political Axis of Party Work in the Industrial Unions," in the political resolution in *New International* no. 4, pp. 23–24 (2008 printing).]

A number of the points in this report are illustrated well in the *Discussion Bulletin* article, "Wearing Three Hats in UAW Local 1200" by Janice of the Detroit branch. She explains that the branch had established a fraction of two in the big General Dynamics tank plant there a couple of years ago. By getting to know the work force and sizing up the union leaders, the fraction had been able to work with other union members, including local officials, not only around struggle situations that developed in the plant, but also in antiwar work, women's rights activities, and solidarity with striking Canadian auto workers and British coal miners. We recruited one co-worker, brought others around the party and YSA, and developed a lot of respect among a broad layer of union activists.

A year ago, the Detroit branch got several more comrades hired into the plant.

"At first we thought this was great," Janice writes. "We mistakenly thought a fairly sizeable fraction could really have an impact on this local, especially in light of the work a fraction of only two comrades had been able to do. But as we went through this experience for a couple of months it became clear that a fraction of such a size was much too large and did not really change what we could do in the local.

"It became a task just to organize the fraction and the discussions we needed to have," Janice explains, "and not to substitute our fraction weight for where workers in the plant were really at in relation to the local. Figuring this out had to do with coming to grips with how our small party can be in touch with workers in other industries through our national fractions."

It's well worth reading the experiences that this

article recounts from our fraction in UAW Local 1200 in Detroit.

Skilled trades

In addition to one-fraction branches and oversized fractions, another problem began to grow up in the party as the result of our efforts to concentrate our forces in the "key sector" of an industry or an industrial union. When we couldn't get hired onto the production line in some auto plants where we thought we needed to have fractions, we decided in a number of branches to organize some comrades to get into the skilled trades.

The problem here is not that these jobs are *skilled*—leave aside how truly skilled they are in many cases. And these jobs *are* production jobs. None of this is the problem.

The problem is that these jobs in auto and in the UAW, as in a number of other industries and unions, have come to make up a big section of an aristocratic layer of the work force—with substantially higher wages, better working conditions, and other relative privileges that foster a greater susceptibility to class-collaborationist and reactionary notions among these workers.

Of course, these branches weren't aiming to keep party members in the skilled trades in auto for very long; our goal has always been to build our fractions among the assembly line workers. From their initial positions in the skilled trades, however, it was hoped that these comrades would relatively quickly find out about job openings and move onto the production line. They could also help other comrades get hired directly onto the line, we assumed. These decisions were made in collaboration with the national leadership of our trade-union work.

A number of branches have tried this route, but it hasn't worked out as planned in any of them. This *hasn't* been the road onto the production line. In the meantime, a number of comrades have ended up working among a relatively privileged layer of workers in the trades departments, with no foreseeable prospect of breaking into where we want to be in the industry. The negative political consequences of maintaining this situation for very long are clear.

The UAW fraction has thoroughly discussed this problem, both here and at its June meeting in Detroit. The fraction adopted a report here recognizing that the balance sheet of trying to build an assembly-line fraction through getting into the skilled trades is that it just doesn't work. The fraction proposed that where we have organized to get comrades into the trades, the branch and fraction leaderships should now help them get into other union jobs as soon as possible.

The UAW fraction is still our largest, with more than 100 members. But it took an important leadership step at its meeting here by adopting a concrete goal to advance the efforts by the entire party to build our other eight industrial union fractions. It voted to take the goal of releasing forty more comrades for transfer to other branches, or to build other fractions in their cities, by the time of the next national fraction meeting in the fall.

Our labor, their commodities

There's another point related to the skilled trades question that should be underlined. As communist workers seeking to unite our class and its allies, we can never give an inch to any notion that workers in certain industries or sectors of industry have some kind of second-class status. We should never counterpose workers in basic steel to those "just working in bucket shops," or oil refinery workers to those working "in some tiny paint factory." We should never start making disparaging comments, even in jest, about workers who "just" produce consumer goods. This is one of those areas where jokes and wisecracks unconsciously slip over into prejudice and aristocratic attitudes.

This results in something akin to narrow craft consciousness, which ultimately comes down to identifying with the employers and their industry rather than with other workers. We can become a little bit "product-conscious," rather than class conscious.

What unites us as a class is not the particular product that each of us takes part in producing, not the concrete type of work that each of us performs. Under capitalism, what we produce belongs to the *bosses*, not to us and our class. We produce it for *them*.

What unites us as a class is that we all have to sell our labor power to a boss. What unites us is the common character of our labor, whatever our particular job may be. The labor of our class is responsible for everything that gets produced. To identify with our boss's product, and to identify other workers with their boss's product (and to denigrate them because of that), raises alienation and commodity fetishism to a grotesque level—and is truly anti-working class.

That kind of attitude can start coloring the judgements we make about building our industrial fractions. We can start bringing into the party some of the backward prejudices that exist in sections of our class, but that have their origins in the enemy class. We can start thinking in terms of "second-class fractions," based on the prevalence of low-wage jobs, or the alleged greater weakness of the union in a particular industry. None of these prejudices hold water when looked at politically. All of the nine unions that we've prioritized are weak today as a result of decades of class-collaborationist misleadership. The ILGWU and ACTWU are no different in this regard from the other seven in any fundamental way.

Every industry and industrial union is increasingly tiered in terms of wages, too. This reflects the progress the bosses are making in their offensive. Take our United Transportation Union fraction in Philadelphia, for example. Comrades there are working on a regional rail commuter system. They hire on at minimum wage, move up to $5.75 during training, and top out at a bit over $7 an hour. This is what the capitalists would like to be able to do to a lot of other rail workers, and workers in other industries as well. That's their aim.

Being conscious to avoid any trace of craft attitudes—of privileged guild attitudes, actually—has got nothing to do with begrudging a few dollars more per hour to workers whose jobs actually *do* entail a longer period of training and extra skill levels, or that are particularly dirty, hard, or dangerous. Most workers will be the first to say that those who've taken the time and effort to pick up some skills, or who have to put up with especially rough conditions, should get an extra few bucks on pay day. That's altogether different from any aristocratic, looking-down-your-nose at other workers because of what they produce, or where they work, or what their wages may be.

Our work in the unions

We need to remind ourselves of how we judge the accomplishments of our nine industrial union fractions. Every step forward we take as revolutionary union politicians, no matter how modest, *is a gain for our unions,* not just for the SWP. We often point to the statement by Marx and Engels that communists have no interests separate and apart from those of the working class. But something more can be said. As communist workers, and as members of the party's nine industrial union fractions, we have no interests separate and apart from our unions. We don't identify the unions with their current misleaders; the unions are institutions of the working class, of *our* class. They belong to the workers, not to the bureaucrats who have managed to get their snouts in the trough.

The nine fraction meetings we've had here register the progress that we're making as a party, and the experience we're gaining in functioning collectively as revolutionary politicians in our unions. I'll list just a few of the many examples that could be cited.

- Our fraction in ILGWU Local 23-25, which includes comrades from the New York and Northern New Jersey branches, recently went through a series of rich discussions with their co-workers around the proposed new contract. The types of questions that came up were explained in a couple of articles in the *Militant* earlier this summer.

- The OCAW convention is coming up next week. Our OCAW fraction succeeded in helping to win a few delegates to oppose the top officialdom's proposed merger with the Paperworkers Union, which would weaken OCAW. Our fraction used some of the literature that had been produced by a section of the officialdom who oppose this merger for some of the right reasons. The main results of the merger will not only be to fatten the treasury of the officials, insuring hefty increases in their salaries and pensions, but also to impose a new constitution for the merged union that eliminates many of the relatively more democratic procedures that exist in the current OCAW constitution. Despite the pronouncements of some of these antimerger officials, of course, OCAW is not by any means a democratic union run by the rank and file. But the ranks do have a stake in defending the gains they have won in exerting some control over our union. Our fraction is part of that fight.

- A member of our New York-New Jersey UTU fraction recently sold a copy of the *Militant* to a co-worker. That issue contained the centerspread article on the contract talks in rail, which explained clearly and concretely why UTU members right now are facing the biggest takeback and concession assault since World War II. After reading the article and being inspired by the class-struggle perspective it laid out, this rail co-worker had fifty copies of it reproduced to distribute at a regional UTU meeting scheduled to discuss these deep concessions. The proposed contract, by the way, was voted down by the UTU chairpeople on a local level in that region, and nationwide.

• Our national IUE fraction just went through discussions in a number of union locals around the new General Electric contract. Their article in the *Militant* explained the different ways that the contract affected workers in plants in Boston, Cleveland, Seattle, and elsewhere, and the different types of discussions that took place on whether to vote it up or down as a result. Each of our local IUE fractions had to figure out concretely how to present a common political approach in quite different situations.

Building a revolutionary workers' party

By adopting this report, we're reaffirming that we are determined to build *all nine* industrial union fractions as genuinely *national* fractions. We're deciding to work toward achieving the kind of geographical spread that we need in all of our fractions.

We are reaffirming that we want multifraction branches, and that smaller fractions will enable us to function more effectively as revolutionary union politicians.

We want to build fractions in a range of different types of work places, among many different types of industrial workers. This includes workers who are very new to this country; who bring into the U.S. labor movement rich class-struggle experiences gained in Central America and the Caribbean; who talk politics in another language, often in Spanish, and will want to become readers of *Perspectiva Mundial*.

If we make progress along these lines, then we'll be in a much better position to turn outward with all of the different political campaigns we've talked about here at this convention—our antiwar and anti-intervention work in defense of the Central American and Caribbean revolutions; the openings to support the rising struggle against apartheid in South Africa, demanding a total break of all U. S. government and business support to the Pretoria regime and its corporate rulers; helping get workers and union officials to go on the farm tours and labor movement tours to Nicaragua; involving the unions in defense of abortion rights; and so on.

We'll be in a better position to deal with the problems we have on the job as women in industry, and as revolutionary socialists in industry.

Labor solidarity

We'll also be in a better position to pitch in when there is a need to build solidarity with workers in another union who are fighting back against the employers' onslaught. There are a couple of struggles along these lines that are going on right now in the union movement, and I'll close the report on this note.

Our approach to building labor solidarity starts with the unions as they exist today. We don't attempt to substitute ourselves and others in the radical movement for what the unions can and should be doing. Some radicals do take this substitutionist approach, forming solidarity coalitions largely outside the structures of the labor movement. These coalitions can at times draw in some significant forces, and we should pay attention to them when they do. But that's not our approach.

Solidarity will be much stronger when it comes right out of the unions themselves, and that's what we are looking for above all. We can be more effective in helping to build that kind of labor solidarity when we have more genuinely national fractions, more multifraction branches, and smaller fractions.

One current example is the Wheeling-Pittsburgh Steel strike in response to a very heavy attack on the wages and conditions of steelworkers employed by that company. Among other solidarity that has been organized in the labor movement, support is being generated in the ILGWU; the spouses of many steelworkers are employed as sewing machine operators and are members of the ILGWU. Having fractions in the ILGWU is a help to us in building solidarity with the Wheeling-Pittsburgh strikers.

Or take the coal miners' strike against the A.T. Massey corporation in West Virginia. Last Saturday a 400-car caravan brought solidarity and food supplies from UAW locals in Detroit. The caravan was called "Motown to Coaltown." Predominantly white UMW pickets turned out to greet the mostly Black UAW workers from Detroit. Mineworkers President Richard Trumka announced a "Coaltown to Motown" caravan for the Detroit Labor Day parade in a few weeks.

We had a joint UMW-UAW fraction participating in this event on a modest scale, and all the comrades learned a lot. We can look forward to similar developments in other unions as the class struggle becomes less one-sided in this country, as we know it will.

BREAK ALL U.S. TIES WITH THE SOUTH AFRICAN APARTHEID REGIME!

By Jack Barnes

The 1985 SWP convention session the day after the report on "Building the party's nine national industrial union fractions" by Joel Britton opened with greetings from Neo Mnumzana, the representative of the African National Congress to the United Nations. Mnumzana outlined the significance of the sharp rise of the struggle in South Africa at the time against the racist apartheid regime.

SWP National Secretary Jack Barnes then gave the following report on behalf of the party's Political Committee, and at the conclusion of the discussion on these reports Britton presented a summary that is printed as the next item in this collection.

Immediately following the convention, the SWP National Committee discussed and adopted a report by Barnes on "The coming revolution in South Africa." That report is published as the lead article in issue no. 5 of *New International*.

There are times when politics becomes simplified—when what you've been working for, organizing for, and preparing for becomes much more possible to do, and to do effectively. This is clearly one of those times.

It is important for us to step back and think about what has been happening just during this week since the convention began, so that we can have a better feel of what is possible for us to do when we leave here, and what it is that we *will* do.

There has been a change in South African politics since we arrived here a little less than a week ago. The struggle has deepened. The stakes have gone up. Talk of "compromise solutions" with the apartheid regime have become less believable. The modern slavemasters have been put more on the defensive. A new generation of revolutionaries and revolutionary workers have deepened their experience in struggle. And there is every reason to believe that this pattern will continue.

These events have been reflected in public steps by even the bourgeoisies of many countries, all of whom hope to stave off the overthrow of the apartheid regime. Yesterday, the government of Argentina denounced the South African apartheid system and pulled out its chargé d'affaires. Even Pretoria's kindred colonial-settler regime, the Israeli imperialist regime, had to denounce the evils of apartheid. The newspapers have reported numerous other diplomatic moves by various capitalist governments that up until now have maintained normal relations with South Africa.

This pace of events puts a spotlight on our responsibilities in this country. The recent developments in South Africa have resulted in a significant change in U.S. politics, as well. When we left to come here to the convention last week, we didn't know that 30,000 people were going to pour into the streets in New York City in response to an emergency appeal issued by more than 50 unions and other organizations. We had already left before the demonstration of 2,000 in Atlanta, and the one of 6,000 outside the State Department offices in Washington, D.C.

We couldn't have predicted how quickly things were going to open up. But we now have every reason to act on the anticipation that what we are seeing will continue and grow over the coming months. In the face of what's happening in South Africa, every human being in the United States—not only revolutionists, but anyone with a decent bone in their bodies—has the obligation to do everything they can to help accelerate this process.

It has become more difficult for any union in this country not to endorse actions in solidarity with the fight for freedom in South Africa. It is more difficult for any large organization, any group, not to endorse an anti-apartheid protest. And it is difficult to believe that the opening of the school year a couple of weeks from now will be business as usual. More than a handful of campuses will open as "Free South Africa universities" this fall.

We operate on these assumptions.

Because of the new situation, there will undoubtedly be all sorts of protest activities in the immediate weeks ahead. The momentum from what we've seen just in the past day or so will continue to spread. And all these activities will build toward the October 11 anti-apartheid actions that have already been called, as well as the October 19–26 actions against U.S. intervention in Central America and the Caribbean. The fight for a free South Africa and the campaign to break all U.S. ties with the apartheid state will become part of all the activities we're participating in this fall as part of the national Jobs, Peace, and Justice Coalition. This is an opportunity to throw every single thing we have into this fight. That is our decision.

We take this movement as it is. We take the action coalitions that exist as they are. We take the people and organizations who are moving into gear around this issue as they are. We take the union movement as it is, with its structure as it is. We get on board, and do everything humanly possible to advance the understanding about, and active solidarity with, the struggle of the South African people.

Fidel [Castro] explains that the Cuban revolution was able to survive because of the struggle of the Vietnamese people. It was Vietnam's liberation struggle that gave the Cuban people the time to develop their revolution, their economy, their defense capabilities, their political understanding and selfless internationalism.

Today, the people of South Africa are giving the whole revolutionary world a better chance to survive, develop, and fight. What is developing in South Africa is Nicaragua's greatest aid—its greatest ally.

What Neo explained to us a few minutes ago could not be more true. Every organization, every union, every worker, every individual who goes into action for a free South Africa in the coming days and weeks also goes into action for Nicaragua, for Vietnam, for Cuba, for the toilers of the world.

Enormous potential

We must grasp to the end the enormous potential strength of this movement—its breadth and depth. The breadth and depth of support in this country for the great, great majority of a nation that is simply taking their freedom, simply taking their freedom to create a democratic state and to become a nation. No single courageous act could inspire such breadth of support around the world as this struggle by an entire people. No single heinous opponent could arouse the international movement that has emerged with the goal of bringing to its knees this modern slavocracy, a slavocracy with a Nazi mentality and cop machine. That is the reality of the racist apartheid regime. We must grasp what this means, and help carry out the unstinting, uncomplicated effort that can turn this breadth of support into *action* against this outlaw of the modern world.

[Karl] Marx and [Frederick] Engels never tired of teaching that the working-class vanguard must understand that it takes the moral high ground in the great conflicts of the world. It sets the example for the world of how to fight for those who are resisting the horrors that outmoded classes have produced. The key to this developing fight in solidarity with the South African people will not be the exact slogan raised in some demonstration, or who ends up on what subcommittee from some union. The key is for all those who are revolutionists to lead others *by example*. That's what we will go out of this convention ready to do.

The decisive thing in South Africa today is politics—the question of state power. That's the decisive question in South Africa. The fight to establish a democratic state in order to build a nation. It is by accomplishing this that the majority will win freedom, land, labor rights, the wealth of the nation for the nation. Every action, every demonstration, every battle, every martyr's blood feeds into that one goal. The question is not one of economic forms, not the exact social measures that a free South Africa will carry out. The question today is *achieving* a free South Africa, and bringing the entire world to bear to help it come into being. A free South Africa will take care of organizing its own affairs, and it will inspire the whole world in the process.

This is the time for us to have the courage of our convictions and of our observations. We have talked a lot about the U.S. working class, about the unions, about Black America, about farmers, about youth, about women, about everyone among the oppressed and exploited who wants something to fight for, especially after the last five years of being knocked around from this side and that side by the employers and the government. People in the United States who go into action around this issue are not only going into the streets for a free South Africa. They are going into the streets for themselves, for a fight against everything that's being done to them, in whatever way. Every cutback. Every plant shutdown. Every cop killing. Every bombed-out abortion clinic. Every reactionary pressure they've had to face.

We need to keep in mind the brutal treatment that working people have been subjected to in the recent past. How coal miners who work for A.T. Massey, and other United Mineworkers members, are prepared differently to respond to this question today than they were a year or two ago. How coal miners in Britain are better prepared. How working farmers are better prepared. How *we're* better prepared than we were several years ago.

Above all, we have a special obligation as a workers' party in the United States. There is no limit to the involvement of the U.S. labor movement in this struggle, as it develops at whatever pace and with whatever ups and downs. The degree of labor participation will be determined by the courage, the initiative, and the simple decision by unionists to say, in the simplest manner possible, "Our unions should join in this fight. We should endorse this action. Let's get going." There is no other limit.

Break all ties

Our goal is for the racist apartheid regime to become the common target of every working person, of every democratic-minded person, of every progressive organization in this country. Our goal is to force the U.S. government—the reactionary power that ultimately stands behind apartheid—to break all ties, *of any kind*, with the South African regime. To make it an international outlaw. We want to answer the lies, to convince every possible person in this country that this should be done. We want to help convince them to move into action, to see that it is done.

Neo told us about the decisions of the June Consultative Conference of the African National Congress in Lusaka [Zambia]. That is a further demonstration of the conquest of the vanguard of the toiling classes, of the political leadership of a generation that is utterly confident, that is building a movement, a workers' movement that matches up to the revolutionary task before it.

Our task is much simpler.

We're interested in something different from what the U.S. ruling class and its spokespeople are interested in. They are interested in whether there are communists in the leadership of the ANC and the place of the South African communist movement in the events there. We have no interest in these questions. They are fake questions, a diversion for the movement.

Instead, we are interested in explaining that the ANC program deserves the support of everyone, of every working person, of every fair-minded person, of every democratic-minded person, of every person who believes that modern forms of slavery are no longer acceptable to the human race, and that those who practice them must be swept aside by any means necessary. We are interested in explaining that the Freedom Charter embodies the demands and goals of the people of South Africa and deserves the support of the people of the United States. The ANC is leading the struggle in South Africa and it deserves the respect and collaboration of all those here and around the world who want to play a role in bringing down the apartheid regime.

We must assume nothing about what our coworkers, students, and readers of our press know about the apartheid system and the struggle to overturn it. Our task above all is to help get out the *facts*. To explain the truth about the multiple forms of oppression and repression under apartheid, and its effects on the lives of 25 million African, Coloured, and Indian people in South Africa. To explain the truth about the movement in South Africa, about its history and its goals, about the mass organizations that are fighting to bring down apartheid. To explain the truth, which working people in this country need to disentangle all the lies and misinformation they are bombarded with in the papers, on television, and over the radio. To explain, above all, the simple, concrete, week-to-week truth about the living movement unfolding in South Africa.

This simple truth will set millions in motion in solidarity as the struggle deepens in South Africa.

Our aim should be to provide our coworkers and fellow unionists, students on the campuses, and everyone we can reach with *facts*. If ever there were a time to patiently discuss, this is it. And on that solid foundation, to organize and to act. That's what has been opened up by these new developments in the South African struggle, and their impact in this country and around the world.

It is along this road that the battle for national liberation, that the battle for freedom and democracy, that the battle for the world revolution is being fought. It is along this road that a new international working-class leadership worthy of the tasks posed at the end of the 20th and the beginning of the 21st century is truly being forged. And it is only along this road that it can be forged.

I am confident that everyone here joins in pledging to our comrades and our brothers and sisters in South Africa that the thousand members of our movement—of the SWP, the YSA, and our supporters—will do everything in our power to set an example of education and action with all those who are ready to advance the struggle to force the U.S. government to end its reactionary support to—and break all economic, military, political, cultural, and sporting ties with—the racist apartheid regime in South Africa.

SUMMARY TO 'BUILDING THE PARTY'S NINE NATIONAL INDUSTRIAL UNION FRACTIONS'

By Joel Britton

The remarks this morning by the representative from the African National Congress, and the decision by the Political Committee to place top priority on deepening our involvement in the fight against apartheid, help underline some of the key points in this report on building our nine industrial union fractions.

The South African solidarity campaign is exactly the kind of thing that we want our union fractions to be strong enough to do—to respond quickly and effectively to new political situations in this country and around the world. The possibilities to mount a political campaign to isolate the apartheid regime are very broad in this country, including in the labor movement.

With this South Africa campaign, as with everything we do, we start with the movement *as it is*, as Jack [Barnes] explained. Not as we wish it were, but as it is. We've gotten a lot better at this, especially over the past few years. It takes a little practice. But it's crucial to our revolutionary political work—in action coalitions, in the campus movement, in women's rights organizations, and especially in the unions.

Our fractions "operate within the union structures and realities of today, with a clear view of the revolutionary transformation that will occur tomorrow," as the political resolution puts it. If we don't start with the unions as they exist today, with their current leadership and relationship of forces, then our fractions will get a lot of those rude awakenings that we described in the report. We will get unnecessarily frustrated by what we aren't able to do yet. And we'll miss the opportunities to accomplish all that *is* possible.

Our line of march has nothing in common with that of the current officialdom, so there *will* be limits to what we can accomplish.

But there are times and issues around which the two paths can coincide for a time. And workers can come out of this convergence by a different road from the one they entered.

If we recognize this, if we don't start with all sorts of illusions, then there is no reason to get frustrated. We just use our heads collectively and work with our union brothers and sisters to achieve as much as possible.

More often than not, we discover that we've actually underestimated how much can be done right now within the existing union structures and with official union support. That's our problem, not the other way around.

South Africa work in the unions

There are big opportunities to carry out political work around South Africa in the unions today. Every one of the nine industrial unions in which we are building national fractions is on record against apartheid. Just about every union in the United States has adopted a position on this issue. What's more, a large number of unions this year have been involved in anti-apartheid protests through official channels, including involvement by the top officialdom and other officials at the regional and local levels. There has already been a greater than usual degree of rank-and-file discussion and involvement in this fight.

We've gotten a glimmer of the work that our union fractions have been involved in against the apartheid regime at the fraction meetings and in the discussion under this point and earlier agenda points. Now we can respond to the challenge and opportunity opened up by the rising struggle in South Africa to step up this work in the labor movement. We want our unions to be at the forefront in opposing any support whatsoever to the apartheid regime by the U.S. government and by U.S. corporations, including most of those that we work for.

This will be completely tied with our work against U.S. military intervention in Central America; the various fall dates projected by the Peace, Jobs, and Justice Coalition focus on both these issues. More action around either one strengthens the freedom fight on both battlefronts. Moreover, as the representative from the African National Congress pointed out so well, every advance for the struggle in South Africa is an advance for our struggle right here in this country.

Joanne from the Houston branch explained during the discussion the other day about the work around South Africa that the fraction she is in has done with co-workers in their OCAW local. The comrades took the initiative in getting the union local to sponsor an educational program around South Africa. The local invited an ANC representative from the area to come down to the union hall to meet workers and give a talk. That had a big impact on a layer of union members, including a few officials.

The fraction has also carried out other educational work, using not only the *Militant, Perspectiva Mundial,* and *Intercontinental Press* articles, but also the UAW's *AMMO* pamphlet on South Africa.

As Joanne explained, all this work in the union made it possible for workers in that refinery to collect 130 or so signatures of union members on a proposed anti-apartheid resolution to present to the union meeting. She said that these workers probably could have gotten the big majority of union members in the refinery to sign the resolution if they had had enough time. And the resolution will be one of those submitted to the OCAW convention's resolutions committee next week.

A complex interplay takes place around this issue on the job and in the union—among and between Black and white workers, between the ranks and the local officials, and between different levels in the officialdom. Let me cite an example that I know directly.

A few months ago, the OCAW local I belong to had shown a video called "Generations of Struggle" at a union meeting. The video traces the history of the fight against apartheid, including the role of the ANC. It provides quite a rich background to the current developments there, starting way back, decades and decades ago.

Subsequently, the chairman of the OCAW unit at the refinery where I work was overheard informally on a number of occasions making some joking remarks that seemed to be pro-apartheid. He was called on it by members of our fraction and by other union builders, but he persisted. The best that could be said was that the union membership didn't know where he really stood on apartheid.

Subsequently the struggle picked up in South Africa, and the anti-apartheid movement deepened in this country, including in the labor movement. There began to be some education around it in official union publications. All of these developments had an impact in our local.

At one of our most recent union meetings, for example, a member of our fraction introduced a strong resolution against apartheid asking that our union, at its upcoming national convention, reaffirm its condemnation of the racist South Africa regime and step up its *active* opposition to U.S. government and corporate involvement on behalf of apartheid. The resolution proposed that OCAW invite representatives from our sister union in South Africa, the Chemical Workers Industrial Union, to come to the United States to visit OCAW locals and speak about apartheid. This resolution was discussed in our local meetings and was adopted.

As a result of all the things that have been going on around South Africa this year, this particular local official—who had previously been making flippant remarks about apartheid—is now one of the people who join in the discussion at union meetings, making good points against apartheid.

Experiences such as these highlight one aspect of the vanguard political role that Black workers play in the working class and the labor movement. Most Black workers are able to distinguish between the different degrees of backwardness on race questions among some of the white workers, and they're ready to team up with those who are interested in having the union take more progressive stands on questions dealing with racism and civil rights, both in this country and abroad. This is a complex process that almost all of our fractions have experience with where they work.

In my experience, and the experience of most

other comrades that I'm acquainted with, Black co-workers most often deal with racist harassment, or other problems that come up on the job or in the union, by talking them out politically with other workers, and in some cases going through the union structures. It's not very common for such problems to be dealt with by threats of physical action against other workers.

Comrades have reported various experiences where Black co-workers have come forward to defend our rights to express a controversial position on Iran or other questions. Once again, however, these union brothers and sisters generally take quite a political approach to the defense of our rights, just as we do. This is applicable to our work on the job and in our unions around the South Africa question, around sexual harassment, around harassment of ourselves or other workers for political reasons, and so forth.

Probing the opportunities
Our fractions should have a confident political approach in our unions not only around South Africa but other questions, such as anti-intervention in Central America, women's rights, and so on. An approach of working with our co-workers. We should seek to involve local officials, bringing to their attention that these are burning issues among union members, and that the union should do something about them, and not simply in a routine way.

The exact tactics and timing will be different in each union situation, but we should never start by imposing some preconceived limit on what can be accomplished. We use our heads, but we probe the opportunities to the limit. Let's talk it up on the job. Can we get some discussion in the union meeting? Can we get a resolution passed? How about some money for an action, or for a bus? Can we get a union contingent in a demonstration, or participation in a protest meeting? What about an official union representative to a local coalition? A union delegation to a campus meeting? Whatever the correct proposals might happen to be in a particular situation in our city and our union local.

We have more opportunities today than ever before to carry out political work through our unions. As we were building the April 20 antiwar demonstrations, for example, we were able in a number of places to work out of our union halls, collaborating with co-workers and union officials to involve others in the labor movement in the action.

We can accomplish *more* along these lines if we have more genuinely national fractions, and if we have smaller fractions in more workplaces and union locals. Our local fractions are more politically effective when we view ourselves not just as part of a particular union local in a particular plant, but as part of the union in that city, in the region, and nationally; as part of the broader labor movement; and as part of a *national* union fraction and a *nationwide* revolutionary party.

Getting to know the labor movement
It's important for us to get to know more about other union locals over the hill and down the road in our areas. We want branches to build fractions in as many of the nine priority unions as possible. We want to find ways to keep in touch with workers in those unions where we don't currently have fractions. And we want to get more on top of the labor movement wherever we happen to be. That's all part of fraction-building, of party-building, of becoming more effective revolutionary politicians and internationalist unionists in the labor movement and the class struggle in general.

In doing this, we'll meet different types of workers, facing different conditions, having different union traditions, and so on. They'll be doing some things that we can learn from, things that could help us in our own union locals to carry out work around South Africa, Central America, women's rights, or strike solidarity.

One obvious place where this is crucial for us is in our national USWA fraction. We're still outside an extremely important sector of the industry and of the union—the basic steel sector. But by building a USWA fraction in other sectors of the industry, no matter what type of plants we're working in, we're legitimate members of the USWA. We can and do attend the district USWA conferences and mix it up with people from other locals, including in basic steel.

All the other things that party branches do—our plant gate sales, our forums, our work around Central America, South Africa, anti-racist struggles, and women's rights—help us keep in touch with these other sectors of our union and the labor movement.

Progress toward building the nine
The discussion under this agenda point confirms that we've been making progress toward a common understanding of what we must do to build our nine industrial union fractions. Comrades in the UAW have explained the decision their fraction made to help lead this process.

We are making progress in recognizing that it's not just the so-called key sectors of these nine industrial unions in which we need to build fractions—that we want to be in the auto parts shops, in the steel fabricating plants, in the airports.

We're beginning to see the advantages of having multifraction branches. Charlene from the Price, Utah, branch—who has for some time been a member of the ILGWU—correctly pointed to the advantages even for a small branch such as that, where building a UMWA fraction was our reason for going there. We started the Price branch to be in a center of Western coal mining and of the UMWA in that part of the country. But once we get rolling, the same general considerations are true for Price that apply to any other branch, big or small. It's an advantage to be in more than one union—even if this only involves one or two people in a particularly small branch. It helps us understand the working-class movement and makes our branches and our fractions more rounded politically.

We're learning the advantages of having smaller fractions. That is partly a product of the political self-confidence and political homogeneity that the party membership has developed through the experience of the turn over the past six or seven years. We could not have arrived at many of these conclusions, much less begun to act on them, at the beginning of the turn. We had *to reach them* in practice first. But now we *can* act on these conclusions. We're in a position to tap the strength we have accumulated as a party, and begin to function effectively with smaller fractions in more locals in our areas. That's a big advance.

ILGWU and ACTWU fractions
I want to make a couple of comments on our ILGWU and ACTWU fractions. Adopting this report will enhance the opportunities to build these fractions. But we can only do that if we understand that the union perspective is central to both these fractions, just as it is to the other seven.

We're not simply getting garment and textile jobs in order to be part of another layer of the working class—a layer with generally lower wages, more heavily immigrant in composition, more female, and so on. Those are important factors, of course. As comrades have explained in the fraction meetings and on the floor of the convention, we're meeting co-workers not just from Central America and the Caribbean, but from China, Vietnam, Kampuchea, Korea, southern Europe, Africa, and so on. We meet all kinds of people in this sector of the class and in the shops organized by the ILGWU and ACTWU. We learn from their experiences and their ideas. It helps bring a greater sense of reality into the party—including on questions such as how much money millions of people get by on in this country, even if they belong to a union; how they survive; how they deal with undocumented status; and much more.

But our aim in building an ILGWU and an ACTWU fraction is to get ourselves in position to function as revolutionary politicians in these important unions. We're there for the same reason we're in the IUE, USWA, UAW, IAM, UTU, UMW, and OCAW—to advance the historic process of fighting to transform our unions into revolutionary instruments of class struggle. The union must be the *base* of our operation—or we won't be able to function.

Getting the skills we need to hold down a job is one big challenge in building the ILGWU and ACTWU fractions. We often face a most immediate test of the statements we made about our experience to the personnel director in order to get a job in a garment shop. So, getting the requisite skills is absolutely essential. It takes perseverance, political understanding, and just plain hard work. Branch executive committees and jobs committees need to pay concrete, individual attention to this.

It's initially harder sometimes to see the union side of being in an ILGWU- or ACTWU-organized shop, since some of the locals we're in are big amalgamated units that rarely if ever have meetings. But in every case where we have gotten in and really worked at it, where we've gone down to the union hall and mixed it up with union activists, we've found that there is a union life in the ILGWU and ACTWU. It may be different from the union life that we're used to in another union, but we can and do carry out union work in these locals. What's more, if we're honest, the internal life in a lot of the other unions where we're building fractions ain't so hot, either.

Take the largest local in OCAW, for example. It is headed by a president who is Black, who has been supportive of efforts to involve the union in El Salvador and South Africa activities. It's an amalgamated local with units based in different refineries and chemical plants. This local—the largest one in OCAW—has had a grand total of two full meetings with a quorum in the last 10 months! The officials organize it not to have quorums, since they have their own reasons for not wanting too many local meetings.

And that's not so exceptional. We all know about similar cases in other unions.

So it may seem easy to say, "Where's the union?" when we're talking about the ILGWU. But we can say, "Where's the union?" in most other situations where we're working, too. And when we find the union, we find leverage for political action and union-building.

The ILGWU fraction has developed and is developing, and so is the ACTWU fraction. We're doing union work in both of them. We need to discuss out these matters more, clarify them, and move the whole party forward to strengthen these fractions.

Fraction continuity

To build all nine fractions, we're going to be releasing comrades from other fractions so that they can transfer to help strengthen our branches in coal mining areas, get into new workplaces, take advantage of new hiring opportunities in rail, and so on. We're also going to be releasing comrades to go to work in the printshop and to take assignments in national departments.

While we're doing all this, however, we're also going to be building more stable union fractions, fractions with greater continuity. This doesn't necessarily mean that these fractions will always have the same people in them, or that we've got some scheme to avoid the inevitable results of the ups and downs in the business cycle. But we're convinced that we *can* develop continuity of party members working in a given workplace and a given union local over a number of years.

That will only be possible, however, when we're building multifraction branches, with smaller fractions in a greater number of workplaces and unions. That's the only way to develop any long-range, stable continuity of our fractions in the nine industrial unions. If we do that, then we'll be in a better position to maintain national continuity despite layoffs, transfers, and come what may.

We're developing a more concrete, long-range approach to constructing stable union fractions and functioning as revolutionary trade unionists. That's the way we will build our party in the labor movement and recruit workers in the years to come.

Branches and fractions

A couple of final points.

One additional problem about one-fraction branches, especially if almost the entire membership is working, is that confusion easily develops as to what is properly branch business and what is properly fraction business. We start having discussions in the branch meeting that are more appropriately taken up in a fraction meeting, including around some tactical union matters. Conversely, we begin to take up some questions in the fraction meetings that actually should be taken up in the branch; if most of the executive committee and the leaders of various areas of branch work are sitting down together in a fraction meeting, there's a constant temptation to slip beyond fraction matters and start functioning as though we're in a meeting of the branch or branch exec.

Finally, there is no rulebook to help carry out the perspectives we're deciding on by adopting this report. There are going to be all sorts of concrete questions that each branch jobs committee and each executive committee are going to have to take up and figure out.

But we do have a common framework for approaching these questions. We want each branch to build fractions in as many of the nine industrial unions as possible, and not just in the "key sectors," the huge plants.

Detroit is already helping to take the lead. Among the workplaces that they've gotten into, as they've moved to become a multifraction branch once again, is a small paint factory of about 50 workers organized by OCAW. This wasn't a place that had a big banner outside the personnel office announcing that it was hiring. But by probing around and opening their eyes and their minds a bit more widely, the comrades are now building an OCAW fraction for the first time in Detroit.

The former UAW members who are now in this paint factory reported some interesting things about it at a national OCAW fraction meeting the other day. One thing that struck them is that the union meetings take place right in the plant cafeteria, involving everybody, including the probationary workers.

They have found that there is a very strong union tradition there, and that this shows up in the general absence of forced overtime, as well as a high level of consciousness around health and safety questions.

We will find more union situations like this in many branches around the country as we keep the following set of factors in mind: building all nine fractions as genuinely national fractions; not just in the "key" sectors; multifraction branches; and smaller fractions.

PREPARING THE ELECTION OF THE NATIONAL COMMITTEE

By Mary-Alice Waters

This report was adopted by the SWP National Committee in May 1985.

One of the responsibilities of the convention of the Socialist Workers Party to be held in August is the election of a new National Committee.

The Political Committee proposes that this National Committee meeting adopt a number of proposals to guide the delegates who will be discussing nominations in branch delegation meetings prior to the convention, serving on the Nominations Commission, and electing the new NC at the final session of the convention. These guidelines should be presented to the delegates at the opening session of the convention and discussed prior to the election of the Nominations Commission. The proposals adopted by the convention will guide the work of the commission.

We propose:

1) That there be no change in the size of the National Committee at this convention.

2) That the convention use alternate membership on the National Committee, especially the bottom two-thirds of the list, to bring onto the NC a substantial number of comrades who are not currently members. This should include both younger party members who have demonstrated their potential to develop as future party leaders, and comrades who, regardless of age, are currently playing a leadership role in branches and fractions across the country. The purpose is to give such comrades, irrespective of previous membership on the committee, the opportunity to go through a year or two's experience as NC members, allowing the party to further test them as well as benefit from their experience.

3) That we reaffirm and apply our general leadership criteria in the election of the National Committee. By this we mean that the party neither has quotas on the NC for comrades who are oppressed under capitalism for reasons of class, race, or sex; nor do we turn a blind-eye to the reality of this oppression or ignore our responsibility to take special measures to encourage such comrades to realize their full leadership potential.

The process of leadership development takes place daily in the branches, fractions, and in the mass movement. We lead the party by helping *every* comrade carry out varied assignments and learn from her or his experiences. In this framework, we consciously act in such a way as to give special encouragement to working class comrades. This fundamental long-term class goal guides us to pay particular attention to helping comrades of the oppressed nationalities and women comrades to overcome the greater obstacles they must surmount to become confident, rounded, political leaders of a multinational proletarian party. The success of this affirmative action is registered in the election of the National Committee.

These proposals build on, and if implemented will enable us to move forward from, the substantial accomplishment made by our last constitutional convention in August 1984. The delegates to that convention reduced the size of the National Committee by roughly 40 percent. This both (1) brought it into harmony with the current size of the party, and (2) established a committee of a workable size.

That step was a real test of the objectivity and political consciousness of the entire party. The proposal was discussed at two NC meetings, and then adopted by the NC. It was discussed by each branch delegation when it met to consider nominations for the NC to be made to the convention.

Despite the nomination of many more than 50 capable comrades, not one single delegate either in the Nominations Commission or on the convention floor proposed that the committee should be larger than the 50 members recommended by the outgoing National Committee. That single fact clearly indicates how well the party understood and agreed with the need to make the change in the size of the National Committee.

We should note another fact, as well. The National Committee led the party in making this change. We tend to take this for granted, but we shouldn't. Subjectivity, not objectivity, often comes to the fore when questions of leadership "posts" and "recognition" are under discussion. I have seen similar proposals evoke very heated divisions in the leadership of other sections of the Fourth International.* The starting point is not always an objective assessment of the needs of the organization, but often a narrow and subjective response focused on what such a proposal means for me, for my tendency, my faction, my clique.

That was not what happened in our National Committee. The NC responded objectively, thinking of the party's needs, not "me," "my role," or "our committee." The NC said to the party, we will have a better committee and a better leadership structure as a whole, one that better suits the needs of the party, if 50 percent of us, more or less, are not elected to the incoming National Committee. Not because 50 percent of us are no longer qualified to be on a National Committee, but because the size of the committee is no longer in line with the party's needs. In doing this the National Committee members demonstrated one of the most important qualities of leadership—the capacity to see themselves in relation to the party, rather than looking at the party in relation to themselves.

Being elected to the National Committee doesn't make anyone a leader, any more than not being elected to the NC means someone isn't a leader. It's an additional responsibility for those elected. But leadership isn't defined by membership on any committee, or any post. It is how you carry out your assignment whatever it may be, how you organize others to work together, how you help others to become leaders.

Emphasizing that membership on any particular body is not what defines leadership, of course, does not mean that the leadership committees are unimportant or that membership on them is irrelevant. To the contrary, revolutionary centralism assumes a structured, disciplined leadership to politically organize the party. These democratically elected leadership committees have enormous weight, and their functioning is decisive in a Marxist party.

The lead taken by the National Committee to reduce the size of the NC facilitated similar adjustments on other leadership bodies, including branch, local, district, and state executive committees. The decision made by the National Committee last December that we didn't need to continue having several elected chairpersons of the party provided yet another small example of how we approach questions of leadership.

The end of a process, not the beginning

The accomplishment registered in the election of the NC at the 1984 convention was the end of a process, however, not the beginning. It was a turning point, a kind of watershed. The adjustment we made created the preconditions to move forward. We were dropping the curtain on a whole previous period. We had to bring the size of the National Committee into harmony with the size of the party before we could have an accurate picture of ourselves, before we could see where we really were

---

* At the time, the Socialist Workers Party had fraternal ties with the Fourth International, an international communist organization the SWP had helped found and lead since 1938. The Fourth International was forged by communists around the world who fought to continue the policies of the Bolshevik Party and Communist International under the leadership of V.I. Lenin, and opposed the counterrevolutionary reversal of that course by the privileged caste that came to be headed by Joseph Stalin.

   During the 1980s the majority leadership of the Fourth International refused to lead its affiliated parties in implementing the turn to industry adopted at the 1979 world congress, and sharply diverged from the SWP's course of acting on the political importance and weight of the communist leadership in Cuba and learning from the experiences of the workers and farmers governments that had come to power in Nicaragua and Grenada in 1979. By the end of the 1980s the SWP and communist leagues in several other countries, in order to maintain the revolutionary continuity out of which the Fourth International had been formed, each decided to end affiliation to this international organization as it had evolved. See *New International* no. 7, pp. 12–15 (2007 printing).

in the development of the party leadership. We had to take that step before we could once again review, and once again concentrate on implementing, the criteria that guide us in electing a National Committee.

We are not saying that the leadership committees elected at the last few conventions were inadequate. To the contrary, they were the correct leadership committees for the party at that time. The report adopted by the opening session of the convention last year reviews this evolution of the NC in relationship to the party from a different angle than we will be discussing at this meeting, and comrades will find it useful to consider the two reports together.

The last convention was, roughly speaking, the culmination of a substantial period of adjustment and change that began with the turn, some seven years ago. Between 1978 and 1984 we succeeded in leading the overwhelming majority of the party into industry and into the industrial unions, changing the axis and milieu of the party and establishing a new and stable framework for building the multinational revolutionary cadre of a proletarian party.

We accomplished this during a period in which the party was slowly declining in membership under the pressures of a strong and concerted ruling-class offensive against the working class on all fronts. There is now evidence that the departures have slowed down, and that recruitment has begun to accelerate, so that over the last year the two processes have more or less offset each other. That is certainly a welcome development. Before the last convention, however, our leadership structures were too large for a party in the range of 800 to 1,200 members. They were still those of a party in the range of 1,500 to 2,000.

When the leadership structure is out of balance with the size of the party, that inevitably affects our political functioning. Moreover, all kinds of broad leadership questions are simply sloughed over because they are not clearly posed. We were like a person wearing a pair of pants that is three sizes too large. Since the pants are too big anyway, you can put on a few pounds, lose a few pounds, and never have to face up to the facts. When there is a lot of slack, you can avoid taking a hard look at what is happening in the leadership, especially on questions such as what progress is being made in the development of leaders who are Black, who are women, who are newly recruited workers (or farmers), who are young.

Just prior to the last convention we made some real mistakes in a number of branches on leadership questions. We started to abdicate responsibility for *leading* on these matters. We discussed this at the opening session of the convention in August 1984, and began correcting ourselves. A good many branch delegations had simply side-stepped the responsibility of seriously talking out and deciding on nominations for the National Committee.

The National Committee as a whole had not done its job either. NC members in a number of branches had not participated in the delegation meetings, sometimes arguing mistakenly that it would be more "democratic" if they stood aside and let other delegates lead on this particular question.

The result in at least one branch was a decision to not even discuss the merits of various nominations for the NC, nor to rank them, but simply to renominate everyone on the outgoing committee, plus whomever else the delegates thought deserved consideration. The National Committee was thus unwittingly elevated into a "House of Lords," whose members deserved nomination simply because they had previously been elected to the NC. Their performance relative to other nominees was not subject to evaluation by the comrades with whom they were working most closely. This, of course, was not the intent, but it was one result of our getting sloppy, and lazy, on leadership questions. It was one more indication of the pressing need to make the adjustment we did in the size and functioning of the NC.

Two challenges

The leadership questions discussed and the decisions we made at the last convention laid the foundations for taking up the tasks that are before us now. The delegates to the 1985 convention will have to address different questions.

The challenge is not to redress a weakness that has already emerged. That has been the case at some previous conventions, but this year we see no big problems that need corrective action by the delegates. It is more a case of looking ahead to avoid sliding into potential mistakes that would be easy to make, given the pressures of the political conditions in which we are building the party today.

There are two such potential problems that we need to talk out in preparation for the convention.

The first challenge is to avoid drifting toward a frozen National Committee. It would be a mistake, and a real weakness, if we went through several conventions that resulted in little change, little renewal, in the National Committee. This would be a weakening of our continuity.

The second challenge is to avoid drifting toward de facto quotas on the National Committee for comrades who are women and for comrades of the oppressed nationalities. We need instead to continue to implement our general approach to leadership development, including our affirmative action norms. The degree of our success in this leadership development will be registered in the election of the NC.

Both of these potential problems are inherent in the kind of political period we are living through, but this doesn't mean that they are unavoidable. They are fostered by the slow pace of recruitment that we have experienced for a number of years, and by an interrelated factor: we are not living through and participating in the kinds of class battles that accelerate the pace of leadership testing and development.

If you look at the statistics on the ages and dates of recruitment for the National Committee members elected at the 1984 convention, and compare them with a similar breakdown of the NC elected in 1979, you can see some of the relevant changes wrought by the objective conditions we have faced in the last period.

There has been a reduction at both ends of the age spectrum, and both register a weakness for the party to be aware of. For instance we would be stronger if we had more Pearl Chertovs and Tom Leonards.

On the other end of the age spread, you will notice that today there is not a single regular member of the National Committee who is under 30 years old, and there are only two alternates under 30. This is quite a change for us. Even in the 1960s, for example, when an extremely high percentage of the NC was composed of comrades with decades of experience, plus another layer in their 40s and 50s, we always had a component of comrades under 30 on the National Committee.

The statistics also show the major clumps of comrades who joined under the impetus of different upsurges of class struggle and began to accumulate leadership experience in those battles.

There is a layer of comrades on the National Committee who were won to the party in the late 1950s and early 1960s—the generation of the Cuban revolution, the civil rights movement, and Malcolm X.

There is another big layer who joined toward the end of the 1960s and early 1970s. That was the period when the Vietnam antiwar movement was at its height, the Chicano movement and feminist movement were exploding, and a number of local battles over desegregation, busing, and police brutality were on the rise.

There was an upturn of recruitment among Puerto Rican, Mexicano, Chicano, and other comrades of Latin American origin in the 1976–77 period, as the bosses intensified their drive to terrorize undocumented workers and to make non-Anglo workers in general more vulnerable to superexploitation. The efforts to organize resistance to these attacks brought a layer of comrades into the party and gave them broader leadership experience. This is reflected in our current National Committee.

After that, from the late 1970s on, there are no big clumps. Even the two National Committee members who have joined since 1980 are not exactly youth. We recruited Mel Mason and Joe Swanson, not their kids. Not yet, anyway. So they, too, are part of the generation whose leadership experience in the mass movement goes back through the 1970s and 1960s, even though they didn't join the party before the 1980s.

The profile of the YSA today adds another graphic component. The YSA is a youth organization in program and perspective, and in its capacity to intervene and recruit and grow. But in terms of age composition, the YSA is not predominantly a youth organization today. At the beginning of 1985, more than 50 percent of the YSA membership was 27 years of age or older, and almost 50 percent had been in the YSA four years or longer. That's a youth organization in perspective and orientation, but not in composition.

This is not because the party and YSA have been doing something wrong, however. It is not because some other political current is getting a new generation of youth while we are missing out. No, that test is coming. The current age composition of the YSA is simply another concrete indication of the kind of period we've been living through. One way we will know when the class struggle is beginning to heat up will be its reflection in stepped-up recruitment of young people to the YSA.

That's why the openings that do exist—like those around April 20, the farm protests, the South Africa demonstrations on campus and off, and the attitudes of young workers toward such actions—are so important to us. Our ability to respond to these developments and begin recruiting out of them—as reports indicated we are doing—is crucial to the health and future of the YSA and party.

On the leadership level of the party, however, which is what we are focusing on here, the statistics indicate that there is not today a burgeoning generation of newly recruited potential party leaders that, by their very numbers and level of activity, is pressuring the party to make room on the National Committee for new blood. Since there is less pressure from this direction than at some other times in the past, we need to be more conscious over the next few years about bringing onto the committee as alternate members a number of younger comrades who have proven their leadership potential.

No one should be elected to the National Committee simply because they are young. We don't have to go out and hunt for "youth" to nominate. And we have no quota we're trying to fill. If we proceed along the lines we have been discussing since our last convention, with thorough preparation by branch delegations and objective deliberations by the delegates, then whatever nominations are appropriate will come out of that process quite naturally.

What we do have to weigh carefully, however, is the choice we make when we have two nominees, for example, one of whom is 27 and the other 41. The younger comrade may be relatively less experienced and less of a leader today—not yet someone who shoulders the kind of broad leadership responsibility NC members are expected to take. But that is not the only thing to be weighed. If comrades have reason to believe that the experience of serving on the NC for a couple of years might give the younger comrade the little push necessary to advance her or him toward becoming more of a leader, then such a consideration should get some weight. That is in the best interests of the party, since, all other factors aside, the odds are that younger comrades have a few more years of activity in them than older ones. Serving on the NC is an education as well as a challenge. We have to think about the future of the party as well as the present.

Having underlined the need to be conscious about age, it is important to be explicit about another question. Otherwise the age factor will get exaggerated.

Renewal of the National Committee does not take place only through the infusion of new young leaders, and at some conventions that is not even the primary source of new blood. There is turnover among older cadres, too, among comrades who have been in the party for a good number of years, taking on varied leadership responsibilities. There is always a layer who are not on the National Committee, even though they are currently playing major leadership roles in the branches, fractions, or national apparatus.

Probably the greatest single weakness of the NC today, for example, is the degree to which it does not incorporate the real leadership of our branches. A good number of comrades who have been chosen by the executive committees of our largest branches to take on the responsibilities of a full-time organizer are not on the NC. There are other comrades with considerable leadership experience who are helping to organize national fractions, or heading up major departments of our national apparatus, and are not NC members. Of course, that is inevitable—and positive. If the leadership were not broader and larger than the National Committee, we would be in bad shape. But the party gains from assuring that a substantial proportion of comrades such as this who are leading our work today are challenged to take on even broader national responsibilities, and that we bring into our leadership deliberations this range of experience.

All of these factors should be taken into consideration in the election of the alternate members of the National Committee, especially, as outlined at the beginning of the report.

This is nothing new. It is one of the reasons our National Committee is structured as it is.

Regular membership tends to have a high degree of carry-over from one convention to the next, since it is composed in large part of the most experienced national leadership of the party. That does not mean that there are few changes in the regular members. To the contrary, there is always turnover, and at any particular convention the changes may be substantially greater than on the alternate list, reflecting real leadership evolution. But there is something different about the way we use the alternate membership.

The convention often uses the alternate list, especially after the first few rankings, to encourage and facilitate the process of incorporating new comrades into the National Committee. Thus the alternate membership always tends to change quite a bit from convention to convention. These changes do not necessarily mean that someone not reelected as an alternate is no longer functioning up to the standards of NC membership, but that the convention is acting to broaden the experience on this national leadership body among a wider layer of party leaders. Using the alternate membership in this way gives a larger cross-section of the leadership the opportunity to work as part of the National Committee and develop in that process. It also gives the party the possibility to continuously draw on and test potential leaders.

Both aspects of this are indispensable components of maintaining the continuity of the party.

This is important, because we sometimes mistakenly think of continuity as synonymous with the long-time stable leadership role of experienced cadres. But continuity is based on the stable *transmission* of accumulated knowledge and experience, and there can be no transmission without renewal and change, without the intertwining of past, present, and future. Continuity is more accurately like a rope or a chain in which new experiences and leadership cadres become intermeshed with the older, and the threads that are worn or frayed are continuously replaced.

That kind of continuity is both a precondition for a stable and authoritative leadership and vice versa. A stable and authoritative leadership is necessary to assure continuity.

Affirmative action, not quotas

The potential to drift toward a de facto quota system in the composition of the National Committee is also inherent when the pace of our recruitment is as slow as it has been. The party is proud of what we have accomplished over the last decade. We're proud of the very real advances we have made in consolidating an increasingly proletarian leadership that includes a sizeable proportion of comrades who are Black, comrades of other oppressed nationalities, and comrades who are women. This pride expresses itself in a determination not to allow the pressures and difficulties of the current period to push us back on this front.

But it's not a question of will.

If we were recruiting at a faster pace, the process of renewing the cadre that is female, Black, Chicano, Mexicano, Puerto Rican, Asian would also take place relatively normally as part of the more general development of new leadership.

But when the pace of recruitment slows down and the normal attrition of time and age take their toll, there can be a tendency toward conservatism, even unconsciously. And conservatism can inadvertently turn into fakery—into fooling ourselves. We can drift toward not renewing the committee, toward not electing new or younger comrades to the NC unless the percentages remain basically unchanged, because we don't want to start sliding back. But that turns the whole question of leadership on its head, seeing election to the NC as the means of conferring leadership status, rather than as a way that leadership development is registered.

We don't approach the election of the National Committee from the point of view of who is *not* being elected. Even less do we start with who is being taken off the outgoing committee. No one is entitled to special consideration *to stay on* the NC simply because they have been elected before; nor do comrades get special consideration *to stay on* because they are a worker, a female, or Black. If we started doing that, instead of trying to apply our leadership criteria objectively to all nominees, then we would inadvertently foster both the development of a House of Lords, and accelerate the drift toward a de facto quota system within it. Rather than electing a committee that reflects the real day-to-day leadership of the party, we would be filling slots. The end result would be a committee with diminished authority in the eyes of the party.

Leadership criteria

One of the most useful things we can do in preparing the convention is to review some of the things we've discussed and adopted in recent years concerning our leadership criteria. What is leadership in a proletarian party? Together with this report we should reprint some of the reports on this question that we've adopted in recent years, and that guide us today, so that comrades can read or reread them prior to the convention.

Here I only want to reiterate a few basic points that are developed more thoroughly elsewhere. The 1978 report by Jack [Barnes] on "Leading the Party Into Industry," and the 1979 report that I gave on "Forging the Leadership of a Proletarian Party," are especially relevant. [Both documents can be found in *The Changing Face of U.S. Politics*, pp. 154–98 and 199–234.]

First, the National Committee is a *committee*. Its capacity to function as a collective political leadership is what is decisive. When the National Committee meets, do the comrades present bring into the deliberations the class-struggle experiences in which the party is involved? Is it a body that has the "capacity to lead the party in action," as Farrell Dobbs's 1971 memorandum put it? Is it "in step with the party ranks"? Most importantly, is it a body that is capable of thinking out and making decisions on the broadest political and programmatic challenges facing the working-class vanguard?

The NC is judged by its collective ability to politically lead, not by the capacities of any individual. Whether any particular comrade should be elected to the NC at a given convention can be judged only by looking at the committee as a whole in relation to the needs of the party.

Second, the National Committee must be the real national leadership of the party. If the NC is not composed of those comrades who shoulder the broad political responsibilities of leading the party on a daily basis, then over time, it will have little authority. Nothing could destabilize the party and undermine the self-confidence of the cadres more rapidly or completely than if a gap were to develop between the real leadership and the formal leadership bodies of the party.

Another way of saying the same thing is that you don't change the leadership by electing an individual to the NC—or by not electing someone. An election per se doesn't make anyone a leader. It has nothing to do with real leadership development, except as a challenge to shoulder greater responsibility; in that sense it can nudge the process along. But election to one or another leadership committee has to be an expression of a process that has already been taking place for some time—in the branches and fractions, in the mass movement, and in the functioning of the National Committee and other leadership bodies themselves. Otherwise it's a fraud that has nothing in common with proletarian organizational norms.

Of course, no National Committee is ever perfect. There is no such thing. Each committee is the best effort at any particular convention to elect a body of a given size, composed of comrades who have shown themselves to be leaders. It is done anew each convention.

Third, the National Committee is not *the* leadership of the party. That, fortunately, is much broader than the National Committee. It is always possible to select some different individuals at any particular convention and have a good committee. Understanding this is crucial to learning to be objective about the National Committee elections, to have a sense of proportion, as Farrell used to say, about every nomination.

Fourth, while the National Committee is judged by its performance as a *committee*, by its collective functioning, the conduct of NC members as individuals inevitably becomes an element that substantially affects the authority of the committee. Respect for and a close and objective working relationship with the ranks of the party; comradely relations and loyal collaboration with other members of leadership committees to ensure that the elected leadership bodies function; the highest degree of integrity in relations with leaders and cadres of the Fourth International and its sections, as well as other revolutionary Marxist forces internationally—on all these fronts, individual National Committee members set examples of conduct that weigh heavily in the ranks of the party and international movement. They reflect on the integrity of the committee—and the party—as a whole.

That is why the party's resolution on "The Organizational Character of the Socialist Workers Party" is so explicit concerning the leadership standards that the party demands of National Committee members. Members of the National Committee have few rights, but substantial obligations and responsibilities. As the resolution states:

> To build the combat organization capable of leading the masses to power, the party must have as its general staff a corps of professional revolutionists who devote their entire life to the direction and the building of the party and its influence in the mass movement. Membership in the leading staff of the party, the National Committee, must be made contingent on a complete subordination of the life of the candidate to the party. All members of the National Committee must be prepared to devote full-time activities to party work at the demand of the National Committee.
>
> The party demands the greatest sacrifices of its members. Only a leadership selected from among those who demonstrate in the struggle the qualities of singleness of purpose, unconditional loyalty to the party and revolutionary firmness of character, can inspire the membership with the spirit of unswerving devotion required for victory. . . .
>
> The membership of the party has the right to demand and expect the greatest responsibility from the leaders precisely because of the position they occupy in the movement. The selection of comrades to positions of leadership means the conferring of an extraordinary responsibility. The warrant for this position must be proved, not once, but continuously by the leadership itself. It is under obligation to set the highest example of responsibility, devotion, sacrifice and complete identification with the party itself and its daily life and action.

Fifth, the development of the party leadership demands consciousness, and, like all other aspects of political activity, it must be led. We have to work at assuring the optimum conditions for the development of the leadership necessary for the future as well as today.

A central aspect of this is an explicit norm of "affirmative action" within the party. We take special measures to support and encourage working-class comrades. We pay particular attention to helping comrades who are Black, the big majority of whom, of course, are also workers, given the class composition of the oppressed nationalities in the United States. We take similar measures in relation to comrades who are Puerto Rican and Chicano and Mexicano and Asian. We help women comrades to overcome the even greater obstacles they face in developing the confidence to be the kind of leaders required of our kind of party.

This is not a question of having different standards for young workers who join the party, Black or white, or for women. There would be nothing more demeaning or paternalistic, nothing more corrosive to the political homogeneity of the party on which the mutual confidence of comrades is founded. Moreover, there is no special road to the development of leaders who come from the ranks of the exploited classes of modern capitalist society and those specially oppressed by it.

The heart of the challenge is the deepening of our proletarian attitudes and norms aimed at encouraging *every* comrade to develop his or her potential to the fullest. No one is ever treated with ridicule or contempt, or made to feel "stupid" or uneducated, for expressing their ideas, however faltering or unsure they may initially be. That is the starting point for a communist party, a workers' party—the only kind of party in which those fighting to overcome the limitation imposed on them by capitalist oppression can develop as political leaders of a multinational proletarian party.

I always liked the way Trotsky emphasized this point in a 1937 letter he wrote to comrades here in the United States, taking up the question of proletarian versus petty-bourgeois attitudes to leadership. He noted that leadership in a revolutionary working-class party is not defined by the capacity to be glib with "general formulas and fluent pens," although that is what happens in organizations dominated by middle-class intellectuals, while workers rich in life experience and class-struggle savvy are pushed aside. The first qualification of a leader in a proletarian party, Trotsky insisted, is the capacity to listen, to hear what comrades are saying. "In the first place a good ear, and only in the second place a good tongue," was the way he put it. [See *Background to "The Struggle for a Proletarian Party,"* an Education For Socialists publication, Pathfinder Press, p. 18 (2012 printing).]

Proletarian attitudes and norms of relations within the party are the beginning of the question—and at least 90 percent of the solution—when it comes to creating the conditions in which young working-class comrades, including those of oppressed nationalities, and women can advance as self-confident leaders of our class. That is not the end of the question, however.

There is a special challenge we face to help, encourage, and reinforce comrades whose oppression in capitalist society—and sometimes double or triple oppression—teaches them day in and day out that they are *not* leaders. That is why we pay special attention, and act affirmatively in our branches to give an extra push, to potential leaders from the ranks of the oppressed. Any revolutionary party that doesn't do that is defaulting on its responsibilities.

This is not a moral question, as it is often posed by liberals. It is an objective necessity that flows from the kind of proletarian leadership required today to assure the victory of the workers' and farmers' struggle for power in this country and on a world scale.

Our perspective and norms on affirmative action are counterposed to two alternative roads that are generally destructive in a revolutionary working-class organization.

One is the quota system. We are opposed to quotas in the election of the leadership of our party today—at the same time that we are intransigent on why there *must* be quotas to make affirmative action programs real in virtually every other organization in capitalist society, governmental or otherwise. We generally support quotas in other organizations we belong to that don't have our communist program and organizational norms.

The 1978 NC report on "Leading the Party Into Industry" took up the reasons for this:

Affirmative action is a fake in industry, in education, without quotas. Quotas are the only possible way we can check the rulers, can force them to retreat. It's the only way that we can raise people's consciousness about this.

Quotas are necessary in another arena too. Quotas are needed in the workers' movement. For instance, in various situations in the unions today. Why must we have affirmative-action quotas in the unions? Why must we fight for the establishment of women's committees, for the right of all-Black caucuses and all-women's caucuses to function in the union?

We do it because of the program of the union bureaucracy. It is not a program in the interest of the class. The leadership of the unions is not democratically elected to carry out a program in the interests of the class. One of the ways we can bust this down and change this is by fighting for quotas. . . .

But we do not use the same criteria within the Leninist party. We must remember the differences. The party's program is a revolutionary program. The party's leadership is democratically elected. The only way the party can function is to base every decision on *political* criteria. And the only way to keep the real leadership (in the eyes of the party) and the elected leadership the same is to function in this way. The party is the *conscious* vanguard of the class. These are the decisive elements that make the party different from the unions today, from the other mass organizations of the class, from the future soviets. Remember, we don't advocate all our Leninist organizational norms for any other organization.

So we are against quotas, against caucuses in the Leninist party. But we are for affirmative action in leadership development and advancement. We are for finding ways and means on all levels to advance party leadership experience of comrades of oppressed nationalities, women comrades, young workers. We are for maximizing the pace of that experience, and maximizing the formal decisions that reflect and encourage that experience.

We are also opposed to the informal, de facto quotas that you find in organizations such as the Communist Party. It's inconceivable that a Communist Party convention would elect a new National Council with a smaller percentage of Blacks than the outgoing council. It's part of the CP's whole bureaucratic structure. The facade versus the real leadership, the top-down designation of leaders instead of their democratic selection by the ranks. It's a fake. That's not to say that there are no leaders of the CP who are Black. There certainly are, but when the formal leadership bodies of a communist party are not composed of the real leaders thrown up by the party in the course of the class struggle experiences they are living through, then the entire structure is a bureaucratic fraud, riddled with paternalism and corruption.

If we reject replacing affirmative action in the party by quotas, we also reject replacing it with the myth that there are and should be no special categories. The pretense that leadership selection can be color blind and sex blind is equally destructive to the fiber and morale of a revolutionary party. "We simply elect people on their merits." Whenever you hear that, you know that some other game is being run. That's not the way this society works, and we all know it. Or, "If all other factors are equal, we would choose the individual who is female, or Black." Those kinds of statements are always a coverup for institutionalizing prejudice, protecting individuals who *can't* stand on their merits if other factors are equal.

All of these are aspects of leadership development that we have dealt with numerous times in the recent years. But we have to go back and review them periodically, because they are the fundamentals for us. They are the starting point for thinking out the question—"What is the National Committee?"—and preparing the election of the NC. Our capacity to be objective in discussing, acting, and leading on these kinds of questions is the reason we have continued to move forward in the real development of leadership cadres from the exploited and oppressed classes and from other oppressed layers of capitalist society.

This is registered in the leadership of the party today. But it is not something we can ever take for granted. It must be continuously reconquered in consciousness and in practice.

A fifteen-year perspective

It is useful to take a look at the evolution of the National Committee over the last decade and a half and think about the leadership challenges that have shaped it. The election of the National Committee at each convention is an eminently political action, and the leadership questions facing the delegates are not static. They evolve as the party itself changes from year to year and as the class struggle poses new challenges to which the party responds.

Following the 1971 convention Farrell Dobbs, who was then the national secretary, prepared a "Memorandum on the Leadership Question" that began with the summary statement: "Little progress was made at the last party convention in carrying forward the necessary transitions in leadership."

That was precisely the challenge facing the party in 1971. For almost a decade we had been recruiting steadily among the youth who were radicalizing in response to the mass civil rights movement, the Cuban revolution, and in opposition to the war in Vietnam. By 1970, the pace of that recruitment had begun to accelerate significantly. A new generation of cadres was coming forward, taking on an increasing burden of the day-to-day responsibilities—in the mass movement and the party apparatus as well. But there was a growing gap between this reality and the composition of the National Committee.

In his usual pedagogical manner, Farrell noted that of the 28 regular members of the outgoing committee, 27 had stood for reelection and been returned to the committee. Thus only one new comrade had been incorporated as a regular member. Five of the alternates elected were new to the committee, but even this had been accomplished by not reelecting four relatively young comrades who had previously served on the NC. The ranking of alternates shifted somewhat, with younger comrades moving up and older comrades down.

That, Farrell noted, did not add up to an adequate pace of transition, and it was up to the National Committee to take the lead in advancing this process more rapidly.

It's interesting to note, for the purposes of comparison later on, that of the National Committee elected in 1971 only 17 percent were women, although the party was 37 percent female. It took a number of years for the rise of the feminist movement and the accelerated recruitment of women to be registered in the National Committee. Seven percent of the National Committee (and four-and-a-half percent of the party) were comrades who were Black. One percent of the members and five percent of the National Committee were Latino.

In the early 1970s the task of organizing and assuring the transition in leadership was our central challenge. It posed some problems that were unique in the history of the revolutionary workers' movement, and we succeeded in meeting them.

We avoided the destructiveness of a "youth revolt" that would have eroded our foundations, warped our continuity, and profoundly miseducated the young cadres on all questions of leadership. That is what happened in a number of sections of the Fourth International. This is one of the things Farrell was always good on. He understood better than anyone the strengths and weaknesses of the party leadership, and he more than anyone was decisive in leading the older generations of cadres to make the difficult transition of relinquishing day-to-day political and organizational responsibility as younger comrades proved capable of taking it on. None of the older cadres ever doubted where Farrell stood on that or were willing to challenge his lead.

At the same time, however, Farrell always made it clear that he would fight—and there is no doubt we would have defeated—any "young turks rebellion." He was determined to *lead* a transition, so that the rope of continuity we talked about earlier would not be severed, with all the negative consequences that would have had for the party.

Because of the strengths of the party leadership, we made it through the decade of the 1970s and into the 1980s before any section of older cadres tried to claim the mantle of age to justify refusal to be disciplined unless the majority did things their way, supposedly the "old way."

It's important to bear in mind that the split that came to a head in 1982–83 was, in part, a split we had prevented year after year throughout the 1970s as we made the transition in leadership and carried out the turn. As the final section of the political resolution explains, the turn to the industrial unions and our orientation to the revolutionary leaderships in Central America and the Caribbean are steps toward building the kind of party that we set out to construct from our founding more than half a century ago—a party that is a living organism, not an ossified sect, responding to and advancing with our class on a world scale. We split with a layer of comrades who did not feel at home, or no longer felt at home, in that kind of proletarian party.

Farrell always used to insist that when the party was finally able to begin to break out of the semisectarian existence imposed on us by our forced isolation from the labor movement, many of the cadres who would find it hardest to orient themselves politically in the working-class struggles of the 1980s would be those whose concept of union work derived from their experiences in the unions in the 1940s and 1950s. Some would become an obstacle to reknitting our communist continuity back through the Teamsters battles of the 1930s, and to relearning how a party of worker-bolsheviks acts to lead the vanguard of our class.

But the transition in the early and mid-1970s and the turn at the end of that decade were accomplished without a split within the political cadre that had led the party for decades. Nor was there any split along generational lines. When some individuals who left the party last year tried to turn it into an "old timers" revolt, it was too late. The split that Farrell always knew was inevitable could no longer damage the party, because we had *made* the transition in leadership. We had carried through the turn before the split developed. The "old timers" scam proved a fiasco, as the older cadres themselves divided and the bulk of the comrades over 50 remained with the party either as members or sympathizers.

A period of rapid change

The 1971 memorandum prepared by Farrell, the reports and discussion in the National Committee, and other leadership moves had an impact. The 1973 convention made some progress, incorporating five new regular members and 13 new alternate members on the National Committee.

In 1975, the convention took a bigger step. The National Committee recommended and the delegates concurred with the proposal to eliminate the category of advisory members of the National Committee. Advisory membership had been established in 1963 in order to open up room on the regular National Committee as the generation of Jim Cannon and Ray Dunne and a few other longtime party leaders who were regular members of the NC retired from day-to-day national leadership responsibilities.

It proved a useful vehicle for a period, but in 1975 the Political Committee recommended that the time had come to end it, and the National Committee unanimously concurred. A permanent "upper house" of the National Committee, composed of members with few responsibilities but all the rights of NC members, was not a desirable institution. It was a temporary measure to meet an extraordinary situation. It had accomplished its purpose and should be ended.

None of the nine advisory members in 1975 stood for election as regular members, and the convention decided to expand the number of regular and alternate National Committee members by ten. The alternate list was used to bring on 14 comrades who were not on the previous NC. The Nominations Commission report to the convention that year quoted from a 1946 letter of Cannon's, and noted that it had been guided by his admonition that the NC should not be a body from which members are removed only with a chisel. It should not be unusual, the Nominations Commission noted, for a comrade to be elected as an alternate member of the NC, to serve in that capacity for several years, to go off the NC for a period, and then perhaps be reelected at a subsequent convention.

In 1975, 1976, and 1977 we had three conventions in a row, each of which expanded the size of the National Committee. That was the period of the most rapid growth of the party, topping out at roughly 1,700 members and provisional members near the end of 1977.

In 1976 the delegates expanded the number of regular members of the NC by three. The committee elected that year registered the leadership development that had taken place among the young cadres who had not only demonstrated branch leadership, but were also veterans of the national leadership of the Boston desegregation struggle and the building of the National Student Coalition Against Racism [NSCAR].

The 1977 convention decided on a further substantial expansion of the National Committee. The Nominations Commission, following the general lead given by the National Committee, proposed an expansion of sixteen; and then the convention delegates, after some discussion, decided to add another five alternates.

The discussion on the election of the National Committee at that convention, however, as we noted in the report adopted in 1978, was so seriously off base politically that it was a warning sign. It alerted us to the need to clarify our leadership norms and criteria, have a thorough leadership discussion, and confront the pressures we were coming under.

The 1977 convention debate headed down two false tracks. On one hand the argument was advanced that there were too many "white males" in the leadership, and that was a problem for the party. It was suggested that the National Committee could be improved by taking off any white male and putting a woman nominee on. The party supposedly had too many leaders to fit on the National Committee, so "white males" should be limited. In the process of sweeping aside the category, a good many comrades carrying major leadership responsibilities in the branches were eliminated from serious and objective consideration for the National Committee, which weakened rather than strengthened its authority.

Secondly, there was an underlying assumption running through the 1977 convention deliberations that electing somebody to the National Committee was the way to make her or him a leader. That is, if we put more comrades who are Black or female on the NC, we will then have more leaders who are Black or female; instead of, if the party succeeds in helping more comrades who are workers or Black or female to move forward as leaders, that fact will then be registered in the election of the National Committee. We were drifting toward having quotas for oppressed nationalities and women on the National Committee under the pretense that this was the way to develop leadership, rather than recognizing that such a course would represent an evasion of our responsibilities.

Another interrelated problem surfaced at the 1977 convention—a "third-world-comrades-only" social was organized one evening there. It was not an event scheduled by the convention. To the contrary, other social activities organized by the convention were taking place at the same time. But the fact of the party was spread by word of mouth. Comrades arriving with companions who were not Black or Latino were told that these convention participants could not come in. International guests of the convention who were of European descent were asked to leave.

As soon as the convention presiding committee learned of this exclusive social gathering, a special point was added to the agenda to discuss the implications of such a thing occurring at a communist convention. The delegates adopted a report explaining why party social events that exclude some comrades on the basis of sex, nationality, race, or language are contrary to Leninist organizational norms. Pointing to the parallel with women's caucuses or gay caucuses, which are by definition constituted on a basis other than *political* criteria, the report explained that such activities organized under the guise of being social gatherings foster cliquism, and are destructive to the party's capacity to cut across the race, sex, age, nationality, language, and other divisions within the working class and forge a politically homogeneous cadre through common experience in struggle. [See "Leninist norms and nonexclusive party social affairs," by Catarino Garza, elsewhere in this bulletin.]

These two discussions, on leadership criteria and on other norms, were interrelated. Disturbing as they were, they were a pale reflection of the destructive battles over these questions taking place in a number of other sections of the Fourth International, to say nothing of other organizations on the left. They registered the political and social pressures the party was under.

These debates burst into the open at the 1977 convention because we had not prepared adequately. The National Committee had not given the necessary leadership in advance of the convention. It was a salutary lesson and we set out to correct that error in the period between the 1977 and 1979 conventions.

At the beginning of 1978 we decided to organize the turn to industry and rapidly began to build several industrial fractions. As part of the turn report we began to discuss all these questions of leadership norms and criteria. We prepared the leadership school and launched its first session in March 1980. We helped lead the fight on each of these questions throughout the International. All this was registered in the character of the discussion at the 1979 convention, the reports on the turn and women's liberation adopted by the 1979 World Congress, and in our capacity to consolidate our gains and deepen our understanding of the leadership questions facing the party.

By the 1981 convention, we again faced a new challenge: bringing onto the National Committee a layer of comrades who had actually led the turn and proved their capacities to lead the party in action. A significant change in the composition of the NC was needed for it to reflect the real experiences of our cadres in the industrial working class and in the union fractions through which the party was being built. The delegates elected a National Committee that included 16 comrades as regular members and 25 as alternates who had not been on the outgoing committee.

Finally, last year, in 1984, as we discussed, the overriding responsibility of the convention was to reduce the size of the NC to make it a workable committee and to bring it into balance with the party. We accomplished that and are now ready to move forward along the lines of the proposals we made at the beginning of the report.

Two other points should be noted, however, concerning the last NC election. As Rashaad [Ali] indicated in the report from the Nominations Commission to the delegates last year, there was one big change between 1981 and 1984. The Nominations Commission found that it was not necessary to give special consideration to comrades leading our industrial union fractions. Leadership there overlapped with other leadership responsibilities to such a large degree, that the commission felt no special measures were necessary. That's a tribute to the success of the turn.

Secondly, the percentage of women on the National Committee went down from 37 to 32 percent. In and of itself, that fact is not a cause for concern. The percentage of comrades on the National Committee who are workers, or Black, or women, or Puerto Rican, or Asian, or Chicano is naturally going to fluctuate from one year to the next. It's inevitable because the class-struggle experiences we live through—both their pace and character—have a powerful impact on our recruitment, on the development of leadership, and on the rate of attrition. That can't help but be registered in changes in our leading bodies. What would be cause for concern is if such percentages didn't change; or if the proportion of comrades who are Black or female always went up but never down; or always down but never up. That would indicate there was something artificial in the way we were selecting our leadership, that we were not being ruthlessly objective with ourselves.

The offensive against women's rights

When we see changes of that character, however, we owe it to ourselves to take a closer look and try to sort out the factors involved. So I want to take the rest of the report to deal with a broader economic and social question that does bear on our recruitment and leadership development: the character of the ruling-class offensive against women's rights and the impact this has had on even the most conscious layers of our class.

This is an important aspect of the pressures that are coming down on us as a small, vanguard proletarian party. The sustained campaign to take back some of the gains women have made is an important barometer of the kind of political period we're living through.

I want to start with one fact. For the first time in nearly 15 years, women constitute less than 40 percent of the party membership—39 percent to be precise, according to the last membership survey in October 1984. Following the rise of the feminist movement at the end of the 1960s and the significant recruitment to the party out of those struggles, the proportion of the party that was female remained remarkably stable throughout the 1970s and early 1980s. The percentage fluctuated between roughly 42 and 44 percent—both when we were growing rapidly and when we were losing slowly.

This was one of the statistics that we watched closely as the party got into industry, as well. We noted the importance of the fact that such a "wrenching turn" had no negative impact on the relative numbers of women in the party. To the contrary, women comrades from the beginning were proportionally represented in our industrial fractions.

So, when the number of women suddenly fell by several percentage points in a six-month time period in 1984, it was a significant development. It is a more important statistic than the decrease in the percentage of women on the National Committee at the last convention, although the two things are not unrelated.

Upon reflection, this should come as no surprise to us. It is another confirmation that we are correct in our political assessment of the character and weight of the ruling-class offensive against the gains of the women's movement. Women are targeted as part of the broad and many-sided assault on the rights and standard of living of the exploited producers, by means of which the owners of capital are trying to shift the relationship of class forces to their own advantage.

The attacks on women's rights are of a piece with the drive to cut wages and social services, lengthen hours, gut health and safety regulations, and increase the rate of exploitation through all the mechanisms at their disposal. The attacks on democratic rights, on affirmative action, desegregation, and other gains of the Black movement; the attempts to intimidate and terrorize undocumented workers; the intensification of anticommunist propaganda as part of the U.S.-organized war in Central America—all these are part of the same large tableau.

As always, however, whenever the ruling class has the bit in its teeth, whenever the bosses are on a stepped-up *offensive* to shift the relationship of class forces in their direction—as they have been for the last decade—women are and must be a special target. It's not just working-class women who find themselves in the line of fire, however. It is women, the second sex.

This attack on women and their rights is fundamental to the success of the capitalist offensive, because it is one of the important ways in which the rulers work to deepen the divisions within the working class. The purpose is to change the way women think of themselves; to weaken and undercut their *class* consciousness as workers; to heighten their consciousness of themselves as women—and not in the feminist sense. The bosses' slogan is "let women be women, and contented with their lot." It's not "let women be workers and lead their sisters forward."

But the goal of the offensive on women's rights is not to drive women out of industry. It never has been—any more than *la migra* is trying to prevent undocumented workers from getting employment. One proof of this is that the percentage of the work force that is female has been rising, from one plateau to another, ever since the beginning of the industrial revolution. The bosses' aim is rather to make women more vulnerable to increased exploitation. It is not to push them out of the labor market altogether, but to push them down.

In a period such as this, the owners of capital need an expanded pool of unemployed workers, an industrial reserve army of labor, reconstituted on an enlarged base. Women have always been an important component. The ideological campaign aimed at women serves to reinforce their tendency to view themselves as only marginal workers, as temporary workers, as a "second" wage earner in the family. Women are supposed to accept unemployment with less resistance and resentment, because they "normally" aren't meant to be working anyway. Aren't their children being permanently damaged by abandonment in childcare facilities, or turning into lonely latch-key delinquents? In periods of rising unemployment, there are always assertions by ruling class "opinion molders" that the statistics are *artificially* high because they include so many women; everyone knows they really shouldn't be counted as unemployed in the same way as men.

The goal is to force women to internalize their dependency, to cause them to blame themselves, not the social relations of production. Rather than demanding as a *right* access to higher-paying jobs in occupations previously closed to them, women are pushed toward being grateful for any job. At any wage.

Part of the strategy is also to break ties and intensify competition between white women and Black women, as well as between women who are fighting their way into nontraditional jobs and Blacks, who constitute a disproportionately large number of the more conscious, vanguard layers of the working class.

The accelerated increase in the numbers of working women, beginning in the early 1960s, was followed by the "second wave" of the women's movement during the late 1960s and early 1970s.

Because of the strength of these advances and the broad changes of consciousness that came with them, the counteroffensive against women's rights in the last few years has been all the more concerted. It has taken numerous forms.

- The defeat of the Equal Rights Amendment [ERA].
- The onslaught against abortion rights—from the withholding of funds to the bombing of clinics. Day in and day out, the propaganda that abortion is murder, murder, murder.
- The glorification of the family, built around women's special fulfillment of themselves as mothers. Supermom is in. She works a full-time job. OK, she's got a right to work. But when she comes home she really makes sure her kids—and husband—don't suffer too much for her selfish absorption in her own life. And, deep down, she really has a lot of doubts about whether she's doing the right thing. Isn't this "new woman" wonderful? How many guilt-tripping articles have you seen like that in the last couple of years?
- The concerted drive to roll back affirmative action gains, to foster the "white-male" backlash against Blacks and women. The goal is not to push women out of the few niches they have secured in job areas previously closed to them, whether it's the mines or the steel mills. It is to deepen divisions and competition, heighten insecurity, promote the idea that women don't really have the right to be there. Since they're taking jobs men ought to have, women are responsible for the high rate of unemployment of Black males, especially.

The counteroffensive to roll back women's confidence and combativity has been registered in the decline of the women's movement. The thousands of small circles of feminist activists have disappeared. The few groups that have survived largely concentrate on specific interests such as health or art. Others have been drawn into reactionary campaigns demanding more cops as an answer to the problem of rape, or calling for censorship laws as the way to deal with pornography. Since 1977 the National Organization for Women has been gutted, turned largely into an electoralist appendage of the capitalist two-party system.

The last time a sizeable women's rights action occurred in this country was 1978—seven years ago. That was the July 9, 1978, March on Washington called by NOW to demand an extension of the deadline for ratification of the ERA. There's been no significant women's liberation action since then, despite the potential that existed around the ERA, especially.

There is no mass fighting women's movement in the streets or anywhere else today. We don't have the kind of movement from which women gain confidence as they fight for their rights, fight to change things that vitally affect their lives. The kind of mass women's movement through which women can, from their own experiences, learn the fundamental lessons of class struggle and proletarian leadership. That doesn't exist today. The women's liberation forces are on the defensive, not the offensive.

This situation is not unique to the United States. It is a general phenomenon that, to varying degrees, marks virtually all the advanced capitalist countries where the women's movement had a significant impact in the 1970s. The reasons for the decline of the women's movement are also fundamentally the same elsewhere, rooted in the beginning of the capitalist austerity drive in the 1974–75 recession, and the incapacity of the current officialdom of the labor movement to mount any effective fightback. Once again it was proven that the fate of the women's liberation movement is not independent of the historic course of the working class, even if it can on occasion surge ahead and help show the way forward.

This is one reason why the abortion rights struggle taking place in Canada right now is important. It's an exception to the general picture. The size and strength and militancy of the demonstrations that have been organized are an inspiration to women everywhere who want to fight, and we should take full advantage of that to educate women in the United States, as well. When our *Militant* reporter recently returned from Toronto and Montréal where she went to do some stories, her first remark was, "I'd forgotten what it was like."

It's been so many years since we've been part of a movement that organized actions of thousands of chanting, singing, fighting, enthusiastic women who felt strong and confident that we *do* forget what it is like. And that is one of the things that is weighing on us today. We are feeling the impact of what is *not* happening as well as what is, and how that affects even the most conscious women.

Pressures in industry are fewer

Women who are full-time industrial workers and part of the union movement are in the best position to resist the conservatizing pressures that all women are subjected to by this economic and political offensive of the ruling class. These women—among whom are most of the women who are members of our movement—have a greater degree of confidence that comes from knowing that they can sell their labor power and survive, thus being able to have some small element of independence in making important decisions affecting their lives. They have acquired at least the beginning of class consciousness through understanding that they have a better chance at improving wages and working conditions by joining together with fellow workers to fight the employer. Moreover, despite the bosses' attempts to foster animosity, women in industry are frequently working alongside male co-workers in job situations where each depends on the other and relations of mutual confidence can develop.

In addition to all these factors, women who are communists are also politically conscious—as workers and as women—and have the advantage of being part of an organized vanguard party that politically orients itself and collectively carries out its work. So party members are in the best position of all to stand up to the pressures on women today.

That does not mean we escape them, however, and we confront them even in industry. We're part of our class, and the offensive on women's rights is aimed at our class above all. We are constantly fighting the suggestions that we're not really workers; that it is a temporary condition; that the important thing is we are women; that women are only a marginal part of the working class; that we are not hereditary proletarians; that we work for a while and then we leave the work force to raise a family; that we work part time or on and off, switching jobs. We're constantly being told that what really defines our lives is not selling our labor power, but home and husband and children.

Because we work with men and women who are generally more influenced than we are by the attitudes and assumptions fostered by the rulers' pervasive propaganda, the truth is that we find it harder today than we did five years ago to simply be ourselves with our coworkers. It's harder to simply be the kind of women (and men) we are: women who are class conscious, political, workers. Communists. Women whose being is not defined by children and family. Women whose interests are focused on being active builders of the revolutionary workers' movement, from which we derive great satisfaction. That's who we are.

We feel more pressure today, from family and co-workers, both, to adapt to conservative attitudes and the backward expectations put forward as the norm by the ruling-class propaganda. We put on wedding rings. We make up stories about kids we don't have. We do all kinds of things.

What we are trying to sort out here is not the element of these kinds of pressures that always surround us, but what has changed over the last five years. That is what is important. And comrades generally feel more on the defensive today in explaining why they *don't* have any children, for example, or why they're *not* married to someone they're living with.

In part this is because party members are, on the average, older, so our friends and associates on the job tend to be older too, and more likely to be married and have families themselves. But it's not only that. Many comrades have had the experience of wondering how best to respond when an acquaintance on the job asks, in a friendly way, if you're married or how many children you have. When it's a discussion between women you often sense that if you say, "No, I'm not married," or "No, I don't have any kids," then you will also have to add something by way of explanation—because the question marks will be all over the other person's face, even if she thinks it's impolite to ask, "Why not?"

When it's appropriate to do so, such questions can immediately get you into a political discussion, as you talk about what you're interested in and what you do with your time when you're not working. But sometimes you just have to try to avoid the discussion.

One thing that we should be clear about is that the pressures women comrades are more aware of today do not come from the turn. We aren't *more* susceptible to the ideological counteroffensive of the ruling class because we are more working class in social composition and milieu. Just the opposite. That's obvious if you stop and consider what kinds of political and social pressures are registered by the "yuppie" phenomenon. If our membership and milieu were primarily middle-class, middle-aged radical and ex-radical professionals and white collar workers, we know what kinds of conservative, despairing conclusions we would be adapting to.

We should also correct another error we have sometimes made in trying to sort out the difficulties facing women comrades in industry. Sexual harassment is a real thing that women have always had to deal with on the job. And it increases in periods like today when the bosses are on the prod. It is one of the issues our fractions need to be constantly alert to, striving to advance consciousness and to win the unions to effectively combat. The reason comrades get hassled and targeted for sexual harassment, however, is first and foremost because we're communists. The bosses want us to quit the party, to quit being leaders. The fact that we are women, of course, gives them an additional way to try to turn the screws on us. But the biggest pressure on the job comes from being a worker-bolshevik. That is what's difficult. Being a woman in industry is not nearly so hard.

The clearest proof of this is that so few women comrades who leave the party pointing to the pressures of working in industry actually end up quitting their jobs. They quit being communists, and then they find that it's really not so hard to be a worker.

Impact on party

Even though women in the party are more conscious than anyone else about the ruling-class offensive and the ways in which women are singled out as a special target, and even though we're more capable of being objective about the pressures we're under as a small working class-vanguard party, we don't live in an isolation ward. The economic, social, and political conditions that surround us bear down harder on women in the party than on men. That is a fact.

There is another element involved, too, and that is age. The median age of the entire party has gone up, and that means the median age of women in the party has also risen. It is a simple fact of life in class society that aging takes a bigger toll on women than on men. Women are taught by all their life experiences, by all the ways they are molded and conditioned in this society, that it is all over by the time you hit 40. You're over the hill. You're no longer of any interest to men. And if you've got a man, you better hold on to him, because you won't get another one.

You're too old to reproduce, so you have no use value anymore. That's another theme we've seen article after article over the last few years—the dangers of having children too late in life. They are aimed at women in their 20s and 30s, and the message is clear. You better have that kid now. If you don't, you'll be sorry, because the likelihood is that any child you give birth to a few years from now will be retarded or deformed. And it will be your fault, because you selfishly wanted to postpone having children until you were too old to produce a healthy baby.

All of this has its impact on women as political beings, and on women as leaders. We've discussed before why women tend to pull back from leadership responsibility, especially from trying to lead men, because they know that few men can tolerate the challenge of women like that. Girls learn early on in life that being a leader will have all kinds of repercussions on personal relationships with men. But the fear of leading, the self-limitation, increases as women get older. It's not always a conscious decision. But the fear of being alone takes on greater weight.

That is why you usually have a higher percentage of women in the leadership of a youth organization than in the party. When you're 18 or 20 you're really not worried about being lonely when you get to be 50 or 60. That's simply a fact. A positive one. You're less inclined to make personal compromises and limit yourself in order to please someone else. You don't put so much store on planning what you hope will be a "permanent" relationship.

These more general kinds of pressure on women in the party are always with us to some degree. But they are exacerbated by the slow advance of the working-class movement and the slow pace of recruitment today. Women aren't carried along by a rising movement. The difficulties seem greater, the solutions fewer, the struggle more protracted.

All these things combined are why we see a small decline in the percentage of women in the party, and why it should come as no surprise.

Given the scope of the changes over the last 40 years in the economic and social conditions women face, it is unlikely that the decline will be large or long-lasting. Women will be centrally involved in every aspect of struggle as working people find the road to effective fightback. This will lead to new recruitment and new leaders coming forward, as well as a new upsurge of the women's movement. But that's not happening yet.

Some parallels with the '50s

In thinking about the conditions we are facing today, it's useful to go back to some of the experiences that the party went through in the period of post-World War II reaction. The overwhelming majority of our members today did not live through those years as conscious political people. Some weren't even born yet. But a better knowledge of the party in this period of our history helps to put some of our experience today in perspective.

The 1980s is not the same as the 1950s, of course. This is not the place to review all the similarities and differences. We've done that in other reports and in the political resolutions we adopted at our last convention.

For the purposes of the questions we're dealing with here, however, we should note that while the ruling class is on the offensive, the political reaction is not so deep. The whole world context is different. Moreover, the changes brought about by the accelerated integration of women into the labor force in the postwar period, and the subsequent rise of the women's liberation movement, have substantially altered the economic and political context from that of the late 1940s and early 1950s.

Some of the things that we are experiencing today, however, are neither new nor mysterious. It's a real political education to go back and look at the ways in which the postwar "feminine mystique" offensive affected the party itself.

One useful thing we can do is to make accessible to comrades today the chapter of party history known as "the Bustelo controversy." The only small piece of the record that most comrades may have read is an article by Evelyn Reed printed in her book, *Problems of Women's Liberation*. It's called, "Cosmetics, Fashions and the Exploitation of Women." That piece is actually an excerpt from a contribution to the SWP *Discussion Bulletin* written in 1954 and entitled, "The Woman Question and the Marxist Method." [The entire record of this debate was subsequently published in *Cosmetics, Fashions and the Exploitation of Women*, Pathfinder, 1986.]

The introduction to the article comments that many of the issues being raised by the women's movement in the late 1960s are not new. It goes on to note that a discussion on the question of cosmetics and fashion took place in the Socialist Workers Party in the early 1950s, and identifies Reed's article as part of that debate. That offers only a hint of the reality, to say the least.

When a sharp division over cosmetics and fashions broke out in the party in the early 1950s, it was not an academic sociological debate. Nor was it a frivolous diversion, despite the fact that it hardly seems to be a question of world historic importance. To the contrary, it was related to the most profound questions of maintaining a proletarian party under conditions of reaction. It would be hard to find a more instructive example of the way reactionary ruling-class propaganda finds an expression within the workers' vanguard, especially when it's under pressure. And the pedagogical way the party sought to bring out the underlying issues is also an education in leadership methods, so it's worth taking time for a short digression to sketch the basic elements.

In 1954 the Cold War and anticommunist witch-hunt still dominated all political life in the United States. The party had just suffered one of the deepest splits in its history, the Cochran split, which cut through the basic leadership cadre, taking a quarter of the National Committee and some 20 percent of the membership.

In July of 1954, a *Militant* staff writer using the pen name Jack Bustelo—whose style many of you will find familiar if you've read much of Joe Hansen—wrote an article called, "Sagging Cosmetic Lines Try a Face Lift." It is a wonderful example of a short, agitational piece of basic socialist education. The article begins by noting how a recession that had just begun was cutting into the cosmetics industry's profits, because women who were unemployed were buying fewer cosmetics. The merchants of beauty had announced their plans to revive profits by convincing women to buy more cosmetics again.

Bustelo wrote: "The Toilets Goods Association reports that after 13 years of steady gains, cosmetics manufacturers' sales suddenly plunged in the first quarter of 1954—right when unemployment took a steep jump." In response, he explained, the big cosmetics dealers were projecting "Operation Big Push." "Toni, for example, has announced its third new cosmetic in three months, a face cream that no words can describe except Deep Magic."

Bustelo then went on to explain what we all know: how the cosmetics industry plays on women's insecurities and fears to try to make us buy cosmetics.

The letters of outrage and indignation began arriving on the *Militant* editor's desk in a matter of days. I doubt that Bustelo was surprised. He probably wrote the article precisely because he knew what kind of reactionary pressures were finding echoes within the party, and his aim was true.

For several weeks the debate took place in the pages of the *Militant*, with letters to the editor and a reply from Bustelo. One reader objected that Bustelo's article was offensive because "one gets the feeling that it is women who are being made fun of." All women really want is "some loveliness and beauty in their lives," the reader argued, but "beauty is predominately monopolized by the wealthy."

"The wealthy are beautiful because the workers are wretched," this reader continued. Moreover, the fact that working-class women strive for beauty "has a progressive aspect, because it is part of the rebellion of women against a position which denies to them part of their rights as human beings."

Bustelo replied with a fine, short essay on beauty, class society, and historical materialism. "I do not believe," he wrote, "that 'beauty is predominately monopolized by the wealthy,' and that the 'wealthy are beautiful because the workers are wretched.'

"It appears to me that you might just as well say that 'morality is predominantly monopolized by the wealthy,' and that the 'wealthy are moral because the workers are immoral.'" The norms of beauty, Bustelo pointed out, like the norms of morals, are determined in the final analysis by the ruling class. And, he added, "I think most of the customs and norms of capitalist society are ridiculous and even vicious, including the customs and norms of wealthy bourgeois women."

To express that view is hardly making fun of women.

Bustelo's reply provoked further outraged responses. Several readers wrote in defending the use of cosmetics as a basic economic necessity for working women to get a job and keep a man. They argued that the party should defend a woman's "right" to use cosmetics.

The last letter printed in the *Militant* accused Bustelo of "third period" Stalinist sectarianism, because, according to the reader, Bustelo advocated "the concept that a woman should be satisfied with ill fitting, poor quality clothing, or that her hair and makeup do not matter because there are more important things." That, said the reader, is the same thing the bourgeoisie tries to convince workers of so they won't demand the same products that the rulers consume.

"Of course," the reader argued, "these standards are bourgeois standards, but they are the norms the women have to meet. . . . If the women want these things, they should have them, and we have to support them in their struggle to get them. . . . It is part of the struggle of women to emancipate themselves from the status of household drudges and to acquire an individuality of their own."

As the character of the divisions became clearer, the Political Committee made a decision to take the debate out of the pages of the *Militant* and to continue it internally. In October 1954 a *Discussion Bulletin* was published containing the letters and critical articles that were not printed in the *Militant*, along with major replies by Evelyn Reed and Jack Bustelo. The full scope of the reactionary pressures coming in on the party are even clearer in this internal bulletin.

A comrade by the name of Marjorie McGowan, a member of the Los Angeles branch, said it all most clearly. She left the party very soon after she wrote her contributions printed in the internal bulletin, and you can certainly see some of the reasons why. McGowan's letter begins by extolling "the revolution in technology and science," which, according to her, had "reached its highest development under capitalism in the last 40 years" and had "wrought a partial revolution in all phases of life."

A revolution has occurred, she argues, "in the relation between the sexes, in sexual morality, in medicine, in nutrition and health, in architecture, in art, in beauty, in hobbies for leisure, in city-planning, in child-rearing, in methods of education, in psychology." This is written from Los Angeles, remember, in 1954.

"These new, progressive and highly creative developments in all phases of life," she continues for the record, can only be finally realized by socialism. In the meantime, of course, "revolution" is changing everything for the better. This is the context for the discussion on cosmetics, because, "What holds true for the rest of life also relates to beauty in the female form."

The revolutionary changes "in the standards of beauty," McGowan states, "flow out of and parallel the concurrent revolution in sexual morality of the last 35 years or so. The long-stemmed American beauty," she raves on, "full of natural vitality and physical grace, with shining hair, clear eyes, smooth skin and natural cosmetics with a trace of accent here and there, is no fiction but an American commonplace. This type of beauty is the American social standard."

It is "an inherent part of every normal female ego to strive toward the preservation" of this kind of beauty, and "this is a proper female goal worthy of the considered attention of a revolutionist."

In case you haven't yet figured out what class McGowan looks to to lead the revolution she's interested in, she eliminates all ambiguities: "There is nothing beautiful in the dishpan hands, the premature wrinkles, the scraggly hair, the dumpy figures in the dumpy housedresses, the ugly furniture and the hodge-podge accessories of the working-class woman and her home."

Not surprisingly, McGowan's espousal of the U.S. imperialist bourgeoisie's racist standards of "beauty," and her contempt for the working class, were accompanied by an open rejection of the historical discoveries of materialists that enabled us for the first time to understand the origin of women's oppression. The Spring 1954 issue of the party's magazine the *Fourth International* had published an article by Evelyn Reed entitled "The Myth of Women's Inferiority," (which is available in *Problems of Women's Liberation*). This was followed by the publication of her "Sex and Labor in Primitive Society" in the Summer 1954 issue of the magazine. Both articles explain that human society has evolved through definite stages of economic and social development and that primitive communism, which was matriarchal in kinship-structure, came first in this historical sequence.

McGowan submitted a long article attempting to refute Reed. She demanded that the editors of the magazine and the party leadership repudiate the views expressed by Reed, which McGowan said were "scholastically irresponsible" and made the party "look ridiculous in the eyes of informed individuals in the bourgeois academic world."

McGowan made it clear that she knew her argument was with Marx and Engels, not just with Reed. She stated her "firm inner conviction that such interpretations of primitive society and primitive social forms as are current in the party today, and have been for the last 75 years or so, are not just accidentally false or innocently misguided."

As Reed noted in her reply, there is "only one interpretation of primitive society which has been current in the party for the last 75 years or so, and which, indeed, we have openly embraced. This is the *Marxist* interpretation, as it was set down by Engels in his *Origin of the Family, Private Property and the State*."

The Political Committee rejected McGowan's request that the magazine's editors dissociate themselves from Reed's positions. "The Political Committee felt it unnecessary to take a position either for or against Comrade Reed's articles," Farrell Dobbs wrote in an October 13, 1954, letter to McGowan. "On such subjects the feeling was that considerable latitude is permissible so long as the author defends the materialist viewpoint, advocates and tries to apply the dialectic method and seeks to supply material of an educational character. . . . From this standpoint, the editors were entirely correct in publishing the Reed articles."

In addition to taking up the challenge from McGowan on historical materialism and the origins of women's oppression—a battle that Evelyn returned to repeatedly over the next 25 years, leaving us with a rich educational legacy that we could be making more use of today than we are—both Reed and Bustelo wrote major articles for the internal bulletin taking up the issues raised by the "cosmetics" debate.

Bustelo's article, entitled "The Fetish of Cosmetics," is a basic piece of Marxist education on capitalism and commodity fetishism, and explains the controversy in the context of economic and social conditions of post-World War II U.S. society. The author's sense of humor makes it all the more enjoyable to read.

Reed's reply also takes up the issues from a basic materialist standpoint: that norms of beauty, like humanity itself, are the historical and changing product of social labor, and cannot be dissociated from the development of the productive forces or from the class struggle.

Reed also deals with the context of the debate in the party, noting that the "past 14 years of war boom and prosperity have produced a conservatizing effect upon the working class which we describe as a 'bourgeoisification.' One of the forms this takes is the readiness of the workers to accept bourgeois opinions and propaganda as scientific truth and adapt themselves to it.

"Like the whole working class," Reed emphasized, "the party is under constant pressure and bombardment from this massive bourgeois propaganda machine." Some of the discussions taking place in the party indicate that "a certain amount of adaptation to bourgeois propaganda has arisen which, although probably unwitting, is a signal that should alert us to the danger."

That is what the cosmetics controversy clearly revealed. "When the comrades defend the *right* of women to use cosmetics, fashions, etc.," Reed stated, "without clearly distinguishing between such a right and the *capitalist social compulsion* to use them, they have fallen into the trap of bourgeois propaganda."

It is true, she went on, that "so long as capitalism prevails, we must abide by these cosmetic and fashion decrees. . . . We must give at least a token recognition of the harsh reality. But this does not mean that we must accept these edicts and compulsions complacently, or without protest. The workers in the plants are often obliged to accept speedups, paycuts and attacks on their unions. But they always and invariably accept them under protest, under continuing struggle against them and in a constant movement to *oppose* their needs and will against their exploiters.

"The class struggle is a movement of *opposition, not adaptation,* and this holds true not only of the workers in the plants, but of the women as well."

Reed also noted a second danger signal that pointed to the pressures the party was under. An important part of the background to the cosmetics debate, Reed commented, was that "for some months an informal discussion has been going on among some comrades on the problem of 'male chauvinism' as it relates to the party. A few comrades have felt that the party itself is not free from this and that women comrades are seriously hindered and handicapped by it."

The Bustelo controversy and the party today

Three aspects of this chapter of party history are particularly instructive.

Even if the objective conditions today are not as difficult as they were in 1954, the ruling-class counteroffensive against women's rights has had an impact on the working class, on women, and on the party. To deny this would be simply closing our eyes to reality.

The division in the party in 1954 over the cosmetics question helps us to understand how pervasive the pressures of bourgeois society can be, and the variety of ways in which they affect even the most conscious vanguard of the working class. We have to be conscious and *objective* about the pressures we're under. We have to strive to separate out the different elements that enter into our personal decisions, and not try to find political justifications or rationalizations for things we do—from the make up we use, to the food we like, to the music we listen to, or whatever.

As Evelyn put it, so long as capitalism survives, so long as the bourgeoisie remains the ruling class, workers will always have to abide by and make some concessions to the economic and social conditions we are struggling to change. But even when we *adapt,* especially when we *adapt*—which we all do all the time—we have to be conscious that this is what we're doing, and not pretend we're advancing the working class along its historic line of march. You don't have to turn make up into something progressive, into a right as opposed to a social compulsion, just because you want to dye your hair so you look younger!

This is also relevant to the decision individual comrades make about whether or not to have children. Nothing could be a more purely personal decision influenced by all kinds of factors, conscious and unconscious. The party couldn't possibly have a political position on so personal a question. But for the same reasons, it's an error to try to find political rationalizations for whatever one decides. Having children is neither more nor less proletarian. It's common to all classes. All the party demands is that we each try to act with as much consciousness as possible, and that we not try to mold the party to serve our personal needs, but to build it as the proletarian vanguard we strive to make it.

If we ever stop being able to be objective about ourselves in relation to the party and our class, then we cease being a vanguard revolutionary organization.

It is useful to consider the "Bustelo controversy" from a second angle: the role of the party in helping all of us to think objectively and politically about the conditions that shape us personally. This is hard to do on our own. Each of us needs to be part of an organized, conscious vanguard party in order not to be just pulled along—adapting, not opposing.

Thirdly, Evelyn's reference to the "informal discussion" on problems of male chauvinism in the party is also important to note. Why did "the woman question," as it used to be called in the workers' movement, became an explosive issue in the party in the 1950s? Not because male chauvinist discrimination unfairly excluded women members from leadership, but because "the woman question" became the banner of the Weiss clique that played a destructive role throughout the real dog-days of the 1950s.

As the party was forced deeper into a semisectarian existence by the objective limitations of the period, as there were few opportunities to turn outward and orient toward intervening in the class struggle, the tendency inevitably developed to search for the source of our problems closer to home. Turning inward and feeding on yourself invariably accompanies periods of reaction. Cliquism, subjectivity, and petty factionalism are fostered by the political difficulties.

Coming out of the Cochran split, a clique in the party led by a member of the Political Committee, Murry Weiss, sought to expand its influence in the party leadership and reduce the weight of the team of comrades that included Farrell Dobbs, Morris Stein, Joe Hansen, George Novack, Tom Kerry, and others. The primary banner under which the Weissites organized to advance members of their grouping in the party—male and female—was a war on "male chauvinism." Comrades such as Myra Tanner Weiss, Clara Kaye, and Frances James were not recognized as central leaders of the party, they claimed, for one simple reason: the male chauvinism of the party leadership. Farrell was considered to suffer the most advanced case of the disease, but every member of the Political Committee—except Murry Weiss—was incurable. The only men on the National Committee given a clean bill of health were, of course, members of the clique.

The goal of the Weissites was not helping women in general to gain leadership confidence, but to advance women—and men—who agreed with them about the character of the party leadership's fatal flaws, its "conservatism." Their campaign was often directed against other women in the party, especially, since the fact that most *women* in the party did not think that Myra Tanner Weiss was a political leader of the caliber her group pretended was a damaging refutation of their entire case.

More than anything, this was a petty-bourgeois clique that directed its attacks on working-class women in the party. Leaders such as Farrell did everything possible to encourage and help organize classes for working women—including working women with children. They, of course, were the party members who had the most difficulty finding time to study. The Weissites, on the other hand, were vicious toward any woman comrade who didn't subscribe to their view of the chauvinist nature of the party leadership. She was labeled "ignorant"—the greatest insult a petty-bourgeois intellectual can imagine—and considered a dupe of the male leaders.

The Weiss clique, of course, generated a counter-clique that also tried to make "the woman question" its banner. Throughout the late 1950s and into the 1960s there were small-scale wars over which women would be elected to the National Committee. There were rather open battles to try to knock one woman off, or get another one on, by bullet balloting, or clique-organized votes to move someone from tenth alternate to fifth, and so on. It was the kind of petty, subjective stuff that is the antithesis of proletarian concepts of leadership. Few things could be more destructive in the election of a leadership body.

But this was all part of the party's forced retreat from proletarian norms under the adverse conditions of the years of reaction and isolation. Comrades who lived through this know very well how destructive it was, and how frustrating it was to be unable to do anything about it until political conditions began to change. It was impossible during that period to have objective discussion in the party on questions of women's liberation.

The Weiss clique itself was destroyed by the recruitment and growth of the party and YSA starting in the early 1960s. Those who were inspired, not demoralized, by the progress and development of the party broke from the clique and turned their energies toward responding to the new openings. The more the party recruited, the more ground the clique lost, the more antiparty they became, and the more they simply withdrew into their private salons to discuss why the party was finished. Some of the Weissites just quit; most were eventually dropped from membership for non-payment of dues. But the legacy of the traumatic battles over "the woman question" hung on, right up to the late 1960s when the new wave of the feminist movement buried it.

The rise of the women's liberation movement brought the definitive confirmation that the party leadership had a correct, revolutionary proletarian line on women's oppression, and sought to encourage women comrades to develop their capacities to the fullest. There was not a moment's hesitation about the importance of that movement or the need to orient the party toward the fullest involvement in it. We were unique on the U.S. left in our response to the women's liberation movement. The Communist Party, the Maoists, the Trotskyist sects—everyone else considered it petty bourgeois, anti-male, anti-Black, and divisive of the working class. And, to begin with, that was the majority view in the leadership of the Fourth International as well. The SWP responded as a proletarian vanguard from the start.

The chapter of party history we've been talking about here—including the destructive way the

Weiss clique abused women in the party and made accusations of male chauvinism their battle cry—was closed with the new rise of the women's movement. We can look at it objectively now and learn from it precisely because it *is* history. If we had a Weiss-type clique in the NC today that hoisted the banner of combating male chauvinism in order to rally people against the party and push their people onto the NC, it would be more difficult to see this period clearly and draw the lessons. The fact that the Weissites operated in the leadership of the party was what gave the clique more appeal and made it more destructive.

In retrospect, it's easy to see how the political conditions created fertile ground for the growth of cliquism. When the going is tough it's always easier to find a scapegoat close to home. The class enemy out there is a big target to set your sights on. It's easier to take on something more modest in size. If the real obstacle to the party moving forward is not the strength and power of capitalism but a handful of men in the party, "them" in the leadership who are mucking us over, who are always on our case, who don't recognize our capacities—that can be a discovery with some attraction for an individual who is getting tired of the hard slugging.

The role of the Weiss clique in the party is one of the purest examples of the destructiveness of such a clique operation in the leadership once it gets rolling, especially when part of its stock-in-trade is hiding behind a campaign to advance the interests of the oppressed.

How well have we done?
The objective weight of the ruling-class offensive on women's rights has been felt quite broadly. But we should note one other thing.

So far we have weathered the pressures of this period as well as any organization on the left, and far better than most. It's helpful to see the SWP in relation to the rest of the Fourth International especially, because there at least we have the common political framework of the resolution adopted at the 1979 World Congress.

Many of the larger sections and sympathizing organizations in the International have lost women from their membership and leadership to a greater degree than we have. We have a higher percentage of women in the party today, and more women who play central political leadership roles, than most other parties in the International. I don't say that with any sense of SWP-smugness. To the contrary, we would be very happy if it weren't true. We don't have "a crisis" on this question in the SWP. Some sections do.

There are three reasons why we have weathered these pressures relatively better than others:

1) The most important is the turn. Making the turn to the industrial working class and its organizations when we did established the political axis and framework of party building for our entire movement. It enabled us to avoid the crisis of perspective and directionless drift that has marked so many other radical organizations the last few years. Within this context, many women comrades played a particularly important role. We gained from being part of the organized union movement. And we were also part of the real vanguard of our class, and of women, when it came to fighting for affirmative action and the right of women to have access to jobs from which we were previously excluded. This gave us some real confidence born of rich experiences as part of our class.

2) The leadership school and education work within the party more generally. The boost of confidence that women comrades attending the school have gained from having the opportunity to seriously study Marx and Engels came at a crucial time for us. The Lenin classes in the party branches have played a similar role for many of us. Again there is a general lesson here that also applies to male comrades, but it has a bigger impact on women's self-confidence simply because we tend to start off with less. The fact that the party is today more communist, more politically homogeneous, affects us all.

In line with some of the earlier points we were discussing, I think it is also useful to note how many comrades, women and men, with children and family responsibilities have attended the school. We took it for granted that we had a special responsibility to minimize the obstacles that comrades with kids faced in getting free for six months, and we organized accordingly. But specially for women with young children, it means even more to have such a chance to study.

3) The basic political grounding and education

of our cadres in a materialist understanding of women's oppression. The standards in the party on this have always been high. No one is ever around the party for long without beginning to get educated on this question, without learning that it is an issue of first-rate importance to the working class.

This is one place, however, where we do have room for improvement today. It's not the purpose of this report to lay out an educational program. We need to think about it and propose a concrete program of study. But it is in order today to step up our educational work on women's oppression, including going back to Marx and Engels, and using more of the things that Evelyn wrote, which many comrades who have joined in the last six or seven years probably have not read.

Back to the election of the National Committee

The report has digressed a ways from its main focus, in order to come back to it with a better understanding of the challenges we're facing. I want to conclude by reiterating the three proposals made at the beginning of the report on the election of the National Committee.

1) That there be no change in the size of the National Committee at this convention.

2) That the convention use alternate membership on the National Committee, especially the bottom two-thirds of the list, to bring onto the NC a substantial number of comrades who are not currently members. This should include both younger party members who have demonstrated their potential to develop as future party leaders, and comrades who, regardless of age, are currently playing a leadership role in branches and fractions across the country. The purpose is to give such comrades, irrespective of previous membership on the committee, the opportunity to go through a year or two's experience as NC members allowing the party to further test them as well as benefit from their experience.

3) That we reaffirm and apply our general leadership criteria in the election of the National Committee. This means that we neither have quotas on the NC for comrades who are oppressed under capitalism for reasons of class, race, or sex; nor do we turn a blind-eye to the reality of this oppression or ignore our responsibility to take special measures to encourage such comrades to realize their full leadership potential.

We have not devoted so much of this report to a discussion of the question of women in the party because we expect—or think we need to accept—that there will be a decline in the numbers of women on the National Committee. There is no reason to anticipate that there will be fewer female candidates for membership on the National Committee. But the party also doesn't make any utopian demands on itself.

We know that attrition takes its toll. Our approach must simply be one of continuing to apply and implement our affirmative action norms, while consciously working to maximize the opportunities for all comrades to stretch themselves as far as possible and take on the greatest leadership responsibilities they can.

As we prepare for the 1985 convention, the key is understanding what we achieved at the last convention, and what that now puts us in a better position to move forward to accomplish.

RACE-BAITING AND COMMUNIST LEADERSHIP
By Mac Warren

This report was adopted by the SWP National Committee in February 1986.

At the August 1985 party convention, during the session at which the National Committee was elected, a delegate from the Northern California Bay Area—who had served on the Nominations Committee and had been nominated by it for the new National Committee—took the floor to express disagreement with the Nominations Committee proposals in relation to two members of the Chicago branch. This delegate was sharply critical of the fact that one Chicago comrade, a Chicano who had previously been a member of the National Committee, was not nominated and that another Chicago comrade, who is Black and had previously been elected a regular member of the National Committee, was nominated this time as an alternate member.

On the basis of these facts, the delegate asserted that what was involved was a "rotten" situation in Chicago, in which comrades who are Black or Chicano are not getting a fair shake because of racial prejudice in the branch leadership.

No more serious accusation could be raised. If true, the charge would require immediate action by the party leadership to make sure the functioning of the branch changed, or, if that proved impossible, to expel the offenders. If false, however, it would also require immediate action—to put a halt to race-baiting in the party.

Race-baiting involves accusing comrades with whom you have a political or organizational disagreement of racial prejudice. It is an attempt to discredit their positions rather than debating them objectively. It involves calling into doubt comrades' motives or character, rather than arguing for or against a proposal on its merits.

Race-baiting is a deadly poison in the party. It makes objective political discussion impossible. It disrupts the functioning of a communist vanguard because it undermines the process of uniting in a centralized proletarian party, by means of voluntary class discipline, workers of different nationalities. Above all, it is an obstacle to advancing the construction of an inclusive leadership, objectively selected, in which the party as a whole can have confidence that each member of the leadership will treat the membership of the party in an undifferentiated way.

Immediately following the convention, the National Committee instructed the Political Committee to find out the facts, take any action necessary to deal with the situation, and to report to the next meeting of the National Committee on what it found, what it did, and, if necessary, what further steps it proposed. The Political Committee assigned me to go to Chicago to see what evidence—if any—existed to substantiate the accusation that the Chicago leadership had put obstacles in the way of Black and Chicano members of the party. If there was none, I was to investigate whether these kinds of charges were undermining objective political relations in the party and were an obstacle to the process of building the kind of leadership we have been making progress on and are determined to continue.

Following this I was assigned by the Political Committee to go to the Bay Area to report to the comrades there on the facts in Chicago. I was also to pursue the possibility that the accusations concerning Chicago—if false—could be an indication of a mode of functioning in the Bay Area itself that had to be changed.

I went to Chicago shortly after the convention. Over a period of more than a week, I met with the executive committee and individual members of the branch and then gave a report to a branch meeting. I asked all comrades for any information that would demonstrate acts of racial prejudice in any way.

Not a single comrade, in any of the meetings I attended or in any of the individual conversations I held, reported anything that could even remotely be taken as evidence that the branch leadership, or the branch as a whole, or any member of the branch, was placing obstacles in the road of the comrades who are Black, Chicano, Puerto Rican, or Asian. I found no evidence of a double standard—one for comrades who are white and another tougher one for other comrades. I should add that the comrades in Chicago impressed on me that they wanted this fact reported to the party because of the accusations that had been raised against them at the convention.

What did I find in Chicago? Several comrades expressed the opinion that racial prejudice in the branch put barriers in the way of comrades of the oppressed nationalities. But when I asked for evidence of this, what they reported did not substantiate the charge. Instead it reflected views about norms of functioning in a communist workers' party that are dead wrong.

The first thing a couple of comrades pointed to was the convention election of the National Committee—the same charge that had been raised at the convention itself. The comrades who raised this disagreed with the nominations made by the branch delegation as well as with the decision of the convention itself. They thought that the comrade who is Chicano and was previously a member of the National Committee should have been elected to the National Committee at this convention. And they thought that the comrade who is Black and who was previously a regular member of the National Committee should have been elected by the convention as a regular member, not an alternate member.

I pressed these comrades for any evidence that these decisions were results of racial prejudice. Had there been any statement indicating that these choices were prejudiced ones? Had some action been taken—openly or not—showing racial prejudice? Was there something more than just the fact of how the election to the National Committee came out? Once posed this way, it quickly became clear that there was no evidence of racial prejudice. Not *any*. There was nothing involved other than a difference of opinion over who should be elected to the National Committee, followed by the accusation of racial prejudice because the party voted differently than an individual wanted.

The second example offered by several comrades as evidence of racial prejudice was the fact that the three regular delegates to the convention elected by the Chicago branch last summer were comrades who are white. (Two of the three alternates were comrades who are Black.) I asked again, what evidence is there that there was race prejudice involved? None was offered. The fact of how the election came out—different from how some individuals wanted it—was supposed to be, in itself, the evidence.

I explained to the comrades that if there was any action taken or any statement made that they could cite to substantiate the charge that racial prejudice was involved in either of these cases, I would immediately take it to the Political Committee and urge, if the facts were proven, that corrective action be taken. But they agreed that there really was no such evidence.

The comrades who raised these points had disagreed with the decisions of the branch on who its delegates should be. They had disagreed with the branch delegation on who should be nominated for the National Committee. They had disagreed with the decision of the convention on who should be elected to the National Committee. That's all. They disagreed. That is their privilege—and we are not going to get into whether or not they were "right" or "wrong." There is no "right" or "wrong" on elections: only individual opinions, individual votes, and the results. But what they cannot do is charge, when their view is not the same as the outcome of a democratic election, that the election is evidence of racism.

It became clear in the course of the discussions in Chicago that some of the newer comrades had drawn their conclusion that racial prejudice was involved from the example set by more experienced comrades, who should have known better. It seemed to be okay—in order to try to get the party to elect the comrades you wanted elected or to assign the comrades you wanted assigned to do something—to raise accusations of racial prejudice to intimidate those who may not agree with you. Race-baiting seemed to be an acceptable mode of functioning in the party.

The charges of racial prejudice were seldom or never expressed openly in the bodies and elected committees of the party. Instead, like all other gossip, these charges were heard most often in the corridors or at social gatherings. Party members who argued privately that comrades who are Black or Chicano weren't getting even-handed treatment never raised this in the branch or in the executive committee, where it could have been discussed and action taken, if necessary. Either they didn't take their own accusations seriously, or—what would be even worse—they didn't take the party itself seriously.

Under these conditions the functioning of the branch and its leadership bodies was weakened. Insinuations about the motives of other comrades on the executive committee made objective functioning in the elected leadership virtually impossible. There was less and less discussion of objective problems and challenges in the executive committee. More and more discussions took place outside the elected committees.

The comrades who felt that such-and-such a person should be elected a delegate, or nominated for the National Committee, didn't try to argue for their proposal in an objective way. They didn't try to persuade other branch members that their nominee was the best proposal for the party. Instead, they abandoned the political discussion.

One of the comrades in Chicago, who is Black, asked me, "What does this policy on race-baiting mean? Does it mean I can't refer affectionately to other comrades as 'white boys'?" I told him yes, precisely, that's part of what it means. It is demeaning to all comrades involved for this to occur in the party. Usually the comrade who is a target of this type of "affection" doesn't appreciate it.

This is crude race-baiting. But it is not the major form race-baiting takes in the party. To focus on the cruder things like this is to miss the more frequent, and more subtle, forms of race-baiting that take place in the party.

Race-baiting is often justified on the grounds of "concern" for the development of leaders who are from the oppressed nationalities. But, of course, that is the last thing it has anything to do with. For one thing, such "concern" over who supposedly isn't getting a fair shake in the party isn't evenhanded. In Chicago, it turns out that only some comrades of the oppressed nationalities were objects of special "concern." Many others weren't mentioned at all, including those who some comrades may feel are equally or even better qualified than others to take on additional leadership responsibilities.

More importantly, race-baiting of any kind is an *obstacle* to objectively taking every step possible to encourage the development of party leaders from the oppressed nationalities. It gets in the way of the development of comrades of the oppressed nationalities into leaders *of the party,* not just leaders of other comrades (*some* other comrades) who are Black, Puerto Rican, Chicano, *mexicano,* or Asian.

What had allowed this situation to develop in Chicago was not primarily some general weakness in the membership. It was a *default in leadership.* Experienced comrades who are Black or Chicano were in a position to call a halt to this race-baiting—and only they could ultimately do it most effectively—but they didn't do so. Some even participated in it. Most of the individual comrades who got caught up in this mode of functioning are white. They used race-baiting to try to influence the advancement of their friends in the party (and of course ultimately themselves as part of an entourage). But this could not have continued if the leading comrades, especially those who are Black or Latino, had exercised their leadership responsibilities and put a stop to it.

There is another side to the leadership default. Many comrades in Chicago thought the race-baiting was wrong. In fact, the refusal of the Chicago branch to allow the race-baiting to determine its decisions was the key thing that eventually forced this situation into the open, making it possible to deal with it. This is a measure of the strength of the Chicago branch and its leadership.

But, looking back on the situation, following the initial discussions while I was in Chicago, the comrades there concluded that they had been too slow to deal with it. Some of the comrades explained that they had earlier thought that to challenge race-baiting would be to cut across the party's political position on the national question itself. They now see how dead wrong this was. Nationalism of the oppressed nationalities is progressive in the United States today. But racial prejudices held by members of the oppressed nationalities—whether toward other oppressed nationalities, toward Jews, or toward whites in general—are not progressive in any sense. They are reactionary.

Unclarity on this is a danger for the party. And it is connected to other questions. For example, part of the explanation for the adaptation to anti-Semitism that was reflected in the *Militant* coverage of [Louis] Farrakhan is rooted in elements of lack of clarity on this very question. When a member of the Socialist Workers Party says, as the comrade in Chicago did, that he sees nothing wrong with using the term "white boy," it is not such a big step to the "affectionate" use of terms like "Jew boy." The two terms are not the same, but there is no giant barrier to prevent sliding from one to the other.

This becomes a critical question when we look at it from the standpoint of the construction of a proletarian communist party in this country, which can only be built as a party that reflects in its composition and its leadership at all levels the nationalities and national minorities that make up the working class.

Sometimes young Black or Latino fighters who are new members of the party express attitudes toward comrades who are white that reflect their experiences with racism in this society. These comrades have not yet thought all the way through the need to build a party of the working-class vanguard. They still haven't reached the point of taking the party completely seriously, and seriously seeing themselves as potentially part of the leadership of the proletariat, across all nationalities that make it up.

Like every member has to, these new comrades go through a process in the party, with the help of the party and through experiences, of becoming rounded communists. Comrades who are part of the oppressed nationalities often have not yet crossed the bridge from nationalism to communism before they join. We all need the party for that. Helping them develop as communists is crucial to the development of leadership of the party. But this means working with them, helping them to become Marxists and communist thinkers and fighters. This includes sometimes explaining what's wrong, or incomplete, in some of their thinking.

If we take seriously these comrades developing as leaders of the party, we will take this responsibility seriously. If we were not to accept this responsibility, and act on it, then we would really be saying something else—that we don't think these comrades are capable of assuming responsibility as part of the leadership of the party. If we were to shy away from trying to convince younger comrades of the oppressed nationalities that, for example, race-baiting is totally destructive in the party and an obstacle to the development of communist leadership, we would be saying that we don't really think these comrades have the capacity to be proletarian leaders. We would be, in effect, setting up two kinds of membership in the party—one for comrades of oppressed nationalities who, for whatever reason, we don't believe can become leaders of the working class and of the party; and one for other comrades who can become proletarian leaders. By doing this, of course, we would be placing the biggest obstacle of all in the road of the development of communist leadership throughout the party.

When these points were raised in the discussions in Chicago, substantial progress was achieved. Most comrades had been thinking about this problem, and across the board there was a receptivity to trying to tackle this task in an objective way. As I said before, the fact that comrades in Chicago had been working to find ways to break through the race-baiting that had become a mode of functioning there was what finally forced this matter into the open, and made it possible for the party to deal with it directly, through the elected party bodies and through the Chicago branch.

Following a report to the Political Committee of the results of the Chicago visit I went to the Bay Area. I met with each of the three branch executive committees in the Bay Area, and gave a report to a combined branch meeting of the three branches. I met with each of the National Committee members and with a number of other comrades individually.

At each meeting I asked the same question that I had begun with in Chicago: Is there any evidence of racial prejudice in the functioning of the party in the Bay Area? What emerged was exactly what had emerged in Chicago. There were no examples of racial prejudice but plenty of examples of race-baiting. It had become an established mode of functioning.

In addition to the kinds of examples that had come to light in Chicago, I learned of others. One of the more important of these was an incident that had occurred at the California state convention of the party in the fall of 1983, in the midst of the split of the minority faction. One delegate to the state convention who was a supporter of the majority took the floor and said that the minority faction was composed of racists. By all accounts, no one at that convention—not any of the National Committee members, not the two representatives of the Organization Bureau who were present, not anybody—took the floor to disavow that charge and explain what is wrong with that method of conducting a political debate. Some of the comrades said they had thought it was wrong at the time, but were not sure how to respond to it.

Another example is equally instructive. In the joint branch meeting in the Bay Area, one of the comrades explained that when she had been assigned to the Los Angeles branch she had complained to comrades in the branch leadership that some members of the branch were racists. She said some experienced comrades had responded, "Yes, you are correct but the party is too weak to be able to do anything about it." Many of these comrades who were accused of being racists were later part of the faction that split from the party.

I asked about the basis for the allegation of "racism" of members of the minority faction. No evidence of racism was offered. Instead, political positions of the minority faction members were brought up. For example, the fact that some members of the minority faction had argued against the decision to build fractions in the garment unions was raised to supposedly back up the accusation. Another example offered was the fact that one member of the minority faction had earlier urged a comrade who is Chicano not to change his name from the Anglo one he had grown up with to an Hispanic name. That was the evidence.

What was involved here? First, on the garment fraction perspective. Opposition to building fractions in garment isn't a racist position. It is an expression of opposition to that path of deepening the party's turn to the industrial unions; and it has been in several of the cases mentioned in California part of a disagreement with the political perspective of the turn. But that doesn't make it racist. What's more, raising the accusation of racism doesn't do anything to advance the understanding of the party on the importance of the garment unions for the future of the U.S. working class and the importance to the party today of building fractions in the International Ladies' Garment Workers' Union and the Amalgamated Clothing and Textile Workers Union. It is the kind of "argument" raised when comrades can't explain a political position. It is a substitute for—and therefore an obstacle to—political clarification. It is a crutch. It is an obstacle to dealing with the real problems of building this fraction and comrades feeling free to present their opinions on it.

Isn't that shown by what happened at the 1983 state convention? Instead of helping to clarify the political and organizational issues in dispute with the minority faction a comrade raised the charge of "racism" as a substitute. It did nothing to educate the party, to advance clear thinking and raise the level and freedom of the discussion—just the opposite.

And what about the question of the comrade's Anglo name? Well, maybe the party member who offered this advice thought that the development of some nationalist consciousness that this name-change reflected was not progressive. It could be that the comrade who offered this advice was wrong on the national question in this country, or he didn't understand it, and was opposed to the party's position on it. And even this is speculation. But if so it doesn't make him a racist. Being wrong on the national question didn't make Rosa Luxemburg a racist. It didn't make Trotsky's positions before 1917 on the national question racist positions. They were revolutionaries. And you can be a revolutionary today and not understand the national question, too. And you can be a revolutionary and understand the national question and not change your name.

Making this accusation of racism breeds something else: pressure in the party for comrades to change their names. "Why don't you get rid of your 'slave name'—aren't you a supporter of national pride?" Experience and getting to know the ANC better has helped us on this. We should have learned by now that adopting a Muslim name, or an African name, or an Hispanic name, is not necessarily a sign of whether or not an individual is an uncompromising fighter against national oppression and race discrimination. The opposite can be—and sometimes has been—the case. And of course the difference between a personal and a political decision and the small but important obligation to mind your own business should be remembered.

To call comrades who disagree with the turn or who don't agree with the party's position on nationalism "racists" is race-baiting. It does not advance understanding of the party's position. It reduces the political discussion to name calling. And it is an obstacle to correcting errors and being more concrete on the turn and the place and limits of nationalism—both of which we're doing.

Race-baiting is a refuge of the politically weak and the cliquist; it is a snare and obstacle for the inexperienced. It turns into a crude attempt—regardless of intention—to advance oneself and one's circle. It diminishes party democracy. It is an obstacle to building a leadership that has the respect of the party as a whole.

This is related to another weakness that we have sometimes fallen into: substituting denunciation of something as racist for looking concretely at developments in the class struggle. Rather than trying to place events into the framework of an analysis of actual class forces in conflict, the shifts in relationships between the contending classes, and the need to intervene with the goal of altering that relationship of forces, we sometimes slip into simple-mindedly denouncing some act as "racist." Instead of analyzing—in order to explain—the forms and mechanisms of exploitation, we sometimes fall back on the term "racist" as though it *explains* that exploitation. Instead of examining the working of imperialist oppression—which includes racism, but isn't reducible to it—we can get lazy and be satisfied with condemning an imperialist action as "racist" as though that *explains* it. This lack of clarity can become a real political obstacle. This is especially the case in organizations that are made up entirely of Blacks, or Chicanos, or Puerto Ricans. Take the National Black Independent Political Party as an example, where being clear on *class politics* is needed for consistent nationalists to move beyond the limits of nationalist positions.

One of the points that I tried to get across to the comrades in the Bay Area and in Chicago is the fact that the cadres of this party take any act of race prejudice in the party seriously—very seriously. The party is more than willing to act decisively to put an immediate end to any manifestations of racial prejudice in this party. We will act regardless of the strength or weakness of a branch. To say that a branch is "too weak" to deal with acts of racial prejudice is, at best, to express complete lack of confidence in the party. This party will not hesitate to act on this—and it would not hesitate to expel comrades if the branch itself won't act on it. Any facts indicating racial prejudice in the party should be brought to the attention of the appropriate leadership body without delay.

However, there is not much fertile ground in this party for racial prejudice. There just isn't. Those who are attracted toward the party are attracted in part by the clarity of the party's stand on this, by its energetic involvement in battles against racial discrimination and oppression, and by the involvement of comrades of oppressed nationalities in all aspects of the party's work and leadership.

But, as our experience has now shown us, race-baiting *can* occur in the party and not be dealt with as quickly as it should be. It is for that reason that race-baiting is a bigger problem than acts of racial prejudice. It was damaging to the party in Chicago. It was an obstacle to the functioning of the elected branch leadership committees. It disrupted the life of the branch—until it was brought into the open and comrades could see what was wrong with it. It gave some comrades who are white the idea that you could fake your way into the leadership by cheerleading for and by being a lawyer for the "needs" of selected comrades of the oppressed nationalities.

The experience of the party, including the discussions in Chicago and the Bay Area, also shows us something else—and something more important. The leadership of the party, including the component of it that is made up of comrades of the oppressed nationalities, is strong enough to deal with this problem. The party leadership includes a significant layer of comrades of the oppressed nationalities. This is true in the National Committee, it is true in the Political Committee and the leadership committees directly responsible to it, and it is true at the branch level. And it is especially true for comrades who are Black.

This is no small accomplishment. What this party has accomplished on this front has never been done before in this country. There has never been a revolutionary communist party in this country with a leadership that cuts across racial lines as much as the SWP leadership does today. In fact, it is our judgment that the SWP is among those parties that have made the greatest progress toward the goal of a genuinely nonracial leadership (in the sense the African National Congress uses the term) of a revolutionary party in the imperialist countries. We haven't finished the process—but we've taken big strides in this direction over the last decade and a half.

And that is why we can have this discussion and settle this problem by eliminating this obstacle to the development of communist leadership. Questions like this one tend to get posed in front of the party as a whole only when they are capable of being solved—not before.

A similar thing happened a decade ago when the question of Black and "Third World" exclusive social affairs got posed, and resolved, by the party as a whole, at the 1977 convention. [See "Leninist norms and nonexclusive party social affairs," by Catarino Garza, reprinted in this bulletin.]

These so-called "social affairs" began to take on the tone and content of a Black caucus and became an obstacle to the development of leaders of the party who are Black. Those exclusive "social affairs" finally came to an end when enough of the comrades who are Black or Chicano or Puerto Rican had reached the point of seeing themselves as leaders of the party, not just as leaders of other comrades who are Black. Enough of us had gotten to the point where we were ready to take responsibility for leading the party. Therefore, we no longer felt we had to lean on the crutch of "social affairs" that were really also political meetings along racial lines.

A tendency toward caucuses of comrades of the oppressed nationalities is almost always present to some degree because of the nature of this racist society. It gets expressed inside the party as a result of the pressures being exerted on the party.

One of the most negative sides of the mode of functioning that drifts toward some kind of "Black caucus" is a simultaneous push away from the comrades who are Black taking more and more responsibility for the leadership of the party as a whole. It tends to begin breeding and reinforcing an attitude of competition between comrades who are Black. It becomes an arena where a two-bit contest—sometimes hidden, sometimes open— over pecking order among the "brothers" and "sisters" rears its head. We would see a situation where development of leadership of Blacks in the party would be seen as occurring in competition with other comrades who are Black. Comrades of the oppressed nationalities who don't go along are themselves badmouthed. We would get concerns over the "pecking order" among comrades who are Black. After all, you would only need so many "Black leaders" to lead the "Black members." Too many leaders would then be a problem. What an obstacle this would be!

Similar points could be made regarding comrades who are Chicano or Puerto Rican or from other oppressed nationalities.

Now we are in a position to resolve this question of race-baiting. If we were to back away from acting decisively on it, it would set us back. If we didn't act, we would be saying in reality that we are going to have a communist party not of equals, but of unequals. We would be saying that some members are going to be allowed to follow different rules, different norms. We would be saying that comrades who are Black or Latino aren't going to be held responsible for functioning under the same standards of membership and leadership as others. We would be saying that there are some comrades who just can't be expected to be communists. They are incapable of leading all sections of the party, all sections of the working class, of having the *same undifferentiated and objective* relationship to *all* members of the party. The standard of personal and political conduct toward the party they will be held to has to be modified, downward, to their level. This is the opposite of the experience of the party the last 15 years.

This would be throwing obstacles in the road of the development of communist leaders who are Black, Puerto Rican, and Chicano.

This would lead the party in the opposite direction from what we have been conquering in the last decade-and-a-half. This would cripple our proletarian orientation and internationalist foundations.

The policy we are adopting today is both possible and necessary to implement. Race-baiting is an obstacle to proletarian norms of functioning, and a barrier to the development of party leadership. It is incompatible with membership in the party.

LENINIST NORMS AND NONEXCLUSIVE PARTY SOCIAL AFFAIRS
By Catarino Garza

This report was adopted by the SWP National Convention in August 1977.

The outgoing Political Committee has discussed a problem, that surfaced at the convention that should be brought to the attention of the delegates, discussed, and leadership action taken.

Since it happened here and news about it will spread throughout our movement, we are bringing it before the highest body of the party, its national convention, so that we can act on it. We think it is a political problem on which educational work must be done.

It began innocently on Monday night when comrades from Latin America and Spain, and Spanish-speaking comrades from the United States, met in a Dascomb Hall lounge. Some comrades from Latin America who had never attended an SWP convention and met so many other comrades from Latin America before, thought it would be useful to organize an informal meeting of Spanish-speaking comrades. They asked other Spanish-speaking comrades to attend and many thought it was a good idea.

The meeting was held during the time allotted for recreation at the cabaret or movies. When the meeting was called to order, it turned out that about thirty or forty people were present. However, the convenors of the meeting had no agenda and had not thought how the meeting should proceed. It was finally proposed that I chair the meeting and I suggested that we hear reports from the different groups present, that we try to keep the reports down to ten minutes, and after the reports we have questions and discussion.

The meeting heard reports from Santo Domingo, Puerto Rico, Colombia, Mexico, Martinique, Spain, Costa Rica, the Latin American community in Israel, and La Raza Unida Party. The reports lasted until almost midnight. Before the meeting adjourned I made the observation to the comrades present that it was like having a conference within a convention. We announced the convention panels on Spain, Mexico, and Puerto Rico for Wednesday and the meeting broke up. Most new comrades felt they had learned something. Some comrades with more experience felt that anyone who follows *Intercontinental Press, Perspectiva Mundial,* and the press of other sections would not have learned anything new. But comrades had been able to exchange addresses, get to know each other personally, and then have follow-up conversations.

Although the meeting was held without any regrettable incidents, this was due in large part to the positive fusion atmosphere in the air. At previous conventions, for instance, such "informal" meetings were used by supporters of Comrade Moreno to begin their underground attack on the leadership of the SWP. They began by calling us racists and gringos, and their attack is now public in a book on Angola in which Moreno accuses Tony Thomas of being a traitor to his race because of the party's position on Angola.* In the future another "informal" meeting of this kind could be used as an arena by someone or some tendency with a particular ax to grind.

A real problem soon grew. I was invited to attend what I thought was to be a social affair of Black and Latino comrades on Wednesday. I have always enjoyed parties and said, sure, my

---

* For more on the political evolution of the current led by Argentine-born Nahuel Moreno (1924–87), see the report "1979: The revolutionary character of the Sandinista National Liberation Front" by Jack Barnes, in *New International* no. 9.

companion and I would be there. My companion is neither Black nor Latina. One of the comrades who invited me indicated that it might not be cool if she attended. Since it was presented as a social affair I didn't think I'd enjoy myself as much as I would at some other social where my companion could also be present and said so.

I should have pressed the matter further. I didn't. That was a mistake.

The social affair was set for Wednesday. But at the meeting of Spanish-speaking comrades on Monday there was an incident that foreshadowed the problems we would encounter on Wednesday. Apparently some individual comrade at the Monday meeting had taken it upon him or herself to tell some comrades that they were not welcome at the meeting. The convenors did not know this. I as the chair did not know this. And the overwhelming majority of the comrades present did not know this. Certainly none of the comrades from Latin America knew about it.

I only found out about it later, when I was asked to prepare this report and began to gather information from delegates and visitors to our convention. The same thing happened on Wednesday night. Comrades of our party and of other Trotskyist parties were "invited" to leave the Black and Latino social on Wednesday night by some comrades of the SWP. This was done without any discussion or decision by the convention, the Presiding Committee, or the comrades assigned to plan and organize the official functions during the convention.

Among the comrades asked to leave this affair was a comrade of the Mexican Partido Revolucionario de los Trabajadores, because he originally came from the United States and is white. He was called a "gringo" by a comrade of the SWP. This is particularly offensive because "gringo" means not just Yankee; it also means stranger, invader. Imagine, a comrade from another section called an invader at a function held at our convention!

This caused some Israeli comrades who had been exiled from Argentina to protest. And it led to the comrades of the Mexican PRT, the Israeli comrades, and some other comrades leaving. They strongly protested the uncomradely treatment of the PRT member.

Another incident at the Wednesday night party involved some Asian-American comrades. One of them is not a party member, but she is married to an SWP comrade who is white, and he was asked to leave. It reached the point where an SWP member was going around the room asking people what their race was and asking people, as it was put, "to respect the feelings of nonwhite comrades by leaving the social."

You heard me correctly. Leninists at a large social affair at this convention went around telling workers of one race that the only way they could "respect the feelings" of other comrades was to get out of the social affair. These are people who in theory are going to go into combat side by side—not necessarily as friends but as comrades in arms who may have to entrust their very lives to each other.

There was even a sign on the door which stated, "Third World Comrades Only!" Whoever it was that took it upon themselves to exclude some comrades from this party never asked the other Black, Hispanic, or Asian comrades of the SWP how they felt on this question.

The organizers of the social affair called me out of the session Thursday to explain what had happened. The initiators of the affair had looked upon it as primarily a way of getting Black and Latino comrades together, to introduce new Black, Latino, and Asian comrades to party veterans, and to help bring them closer to the party in a relaxed social atmosphere.

The comrades who organized the social affair are serious, leading comrades of the party. They were involved in workshops on Wednesday evening and arrived at the social affair after it had begun and after these incidents took place. As soon as they learned about what had happened, they and other comrades present tried to undo the damage that was done. They sought out the comrades who had been made unwelcome and some of them returned to the social affair. However, they were not successful in all cases and some new Latino comrades from branches in the South and Southwest who saw this were angered and disoriented by the attitudes toward white comrades in their branches displayed by other Latino and Black comrades.

In discussing this problem with Willie Mae Reid, she pointed out to me that regardless of the intentions of comrades who organize convention parties that exclude white comrades, such actions create a problem. She pointed out that the same argument could be made with just as much validity for all-women's social affairs at conventions because male comrades sometimes make women comrades feel uncomfortable. She explained that this argument is sometimes used by advocates of all-women's parties. But if we make it a practice for one group within the party to have its own social affairs under what appear to be party auspices, official or unofficial, we miseducate the entire party. To do that would defeat the purpose of our convention and its role in forging the multinational party we need to lead the socialist revolution in this country. That could take place in many ways.

Some of the things that we do at our convention, for example, become the standard for the way things are done in branches throughout the country. We could have branches permitting or organizing social events of this nature on the basis that it was permitted at the national convention and therefore it must be all right. That is not the case. Organizing socials like the one on Wednesday sets into motion a dynamic of its own that cuts across our main objective, the formation of the kind of party we need.

This is a problem that is going to come up at each convention as we continue to grow and to bring into our party more people of the oppressed nationalities in the United States. Capitalist society divides us, by sex, color, national origin, affectional preference, and in many other ways. In the capitalist world we seek to protect ourselves in many different ways. We have Black, Hispanic, and Asian societies, caucuses, different types of clubs, etc.

The party exists in the capitalist world and reflects the pressures society places on us as individuals and as an organization. But the party is not the capitalist world. We *combat* these pressures by conscious effort, but it is an unending pressure. Short of the revolution, and even after the bourgeoisie is replaced, there will be vestiges of capitalist training. Our only recourse is to consciously fight those prejudices that capitalism creates in each of us.

That doesn't mean that all of us as individuals can totally overcome these problems. The party recognizes this and has no rules about who you invite to your home, except obvious categories like fascists and cops. The party doesn't say what kind of music you may listen to, whom you may live with or may not live with, etc. Those are personal relations that the party keeps its nose out of.

What the party can't tolerate is the injection of anti-internationalist conduct into the party or into any of its activities that tend to divide the party along the lines that capitalist society divides our class. It would be disastrous for our purpose.

The question is not new. In Trotsky's *History of the Russian Revolution,* in the section entitled "The Problem of Nationalities," he clearly points out that the party of the Bolsheviks, Lenin's party, never permitted itself to let national feelings cut across the central task of forging the instrument of the revolution, the multinational working-class combat party.

We know that no party in history has understood the problem of oppressed nationalities better than the Bolsheviks. They are our model. They won the support of the oppressed people of the prison house of nations that was Russia by their ceaseless fight for the rights of the oppressed people. However, no party was a more solid fighting unit of the *working class* than the Bolsheviks.

That's what we're trying to create. People who come to our movement must be trained in that internationalist proletarian tradition if they are to become revolutionists equal to history's tasks. That process is long and hard and we must patiently explain to all comrades where divisions come from. We must also make it plain that we won't tolerate any activity that weakens or divides us.

We seek to be a model to other sections of the international in this respect, and we must admit that at this convention we haven't lived up 100 percent to our own standards. That is why we are making this report to you, so that we can begin correcting this mistake. If this report is accepted, the report will be part of the official convention record and comrades throughout the world will read it. There will be no misunderstanding about our position. But more is involved than hurting the feelings of guests here or from abroad. It is a political question and thus a responsibility of the leadership to educate future party cadre.

And this is, above all, a question for the leadership of the party to handle, to lead on. The problems here were not simply the result of new comrades acting out of inexperience. If that were all that was involved, the question would be simple. But the newer comrades and contacts were following the lead of more experienced comrades, and that is where we have to begin the process of straightening this out. That is why we are bringing this report before the convention delegates for discussion and your action.

We propose that no more affairs like the one that took place here on Wednesday, or that excludes any comrade, be organized at our conventions or in the branches.

This is, of course, different from cases where the branch sometimes organizes dinners or other gatherings and assigns certain comrades to attend—for example, a dinner with contacts from NOW, or NSCAR, or the anti-nuclear-power movement, or some other political arena. Naturally comrades interested in or active in these areas of party activity would be the ones to attend.

Such affairs are completely within the normal framework of party activity. What happened here at the convention, however, is not. It cuts across our objectives and similar events do the same. That is why we propose that such "social" affairs cease.

Harry Wicks, Jim Cannon's early comrade in arms in the fight for Trotsky's program, told us earlier at this convention how in Moscow when the Fosterites met and spoke about Jim Cannon, they reminded themselves that "the son of a bitch" was a hell of an organizer.

Comrade Wicks also pointed out that the Fosterites missed the point. That what was really at the bottom of this attribute was Cannon's profound internationalism. That's how this party was begun and it remains our bedrock foundation. Any form of racism or chauvinism among SWP members is a mortal danger to the party. Among comrades, expressions like gringo, whitey, Jew when you really mean kike, can lead to spick, bitch, or nigger. That cancer is a malignancy that we will remove before it spreads. We will maintain our internationalist tradition and build the American Bolshevik party, the Socialist Workers Party.

Summary

This has been a very rich discussion with a wide range of views and experiences expressed. We will incorporate key points from the discussion into the summary and publish it and the report for the entire membership to read and consider.

Several comrades raised questions about what activities the report implies that party members should not engage in. So I think that first of all it's important to clarify what the report does *not* mean.

The purpose of the report is not to suggest that comrades cannot have parties or dinners at their homes or apartments or in their rooms at conventions, and invite whomever they choose. Within the party comrades find friends and socialize with them, and whomever they invite to their homes or socialize with is their business.

Furthermore, the report was not directed to the problems of how to organize better social activities at our conventions. It is clear from the discussion that these activities need to be reexamined, reorganized, and made more attractive for everybody that comes here. We must continue the process we started a couple of years ago of drawing more Black and Latino comrades into the planning and organization of these activities.

Nor was the report suggesting that branches should not organize informal affairs with contacts that are specifically designed to help win them to the party. Sometimes those assigned to attend such gatherings will only be comrades who are involved in or knowledgeable about the area of work the contacts are interested in. In other cases, however, the contacts may be more interested in meeting people involved in *other* areas of work. Auto workers who want to find out more about the SWP won't just want to talk to other auto workers. They will want to meet comrades involved in women's liberation work, South Africa work, our election campaigns, and so on. If they are attracted to the *party,* they are not just interested in a particular arena of work, and they will want to know who else is in the party besides the kind of people they have already met.

These are questions of tactics and judgment that must be left to the branches and locals to work out.

The report concentrated on the *political* problems posed by the type of affairs held Wednesday night at this convention. As a couple of comrades pointed out, regardless of the intentions of the organizers of the affair Wednesday night, the affair turned out to have negative consequences.

The real problem with events such as the Wednesday night "Third World" party was explained by several comrades. That is that they tend to become political gatherings where serious questions are taken up, but in a framework that prevents them from coming before party bodies that can resolve them. The particular section of the membership that gets invited to these affairs and therefore can participate in these political discussions is powerless to make any decisions. That can only be done by the party membership as a whole, or through democratically elected leadership bodies. Thus there is a frustration built into these meetings: a pressure to become sterile gripe sessions.

Another comrade pointed out another aspect of this. Discussions—and pressure—about how Black comrades, or women comrades, should organize their social and even private lives often occur at such events. This kind of pressure about how comrades should lead their personal lives has no place in this party.

As someone pointed out during the discussion, "social" affairs where Black comrades cannot bring white companions can also lead to frictions not only between Black and white comrades, but also among Black comrades. They tend to divide, rather than unite, the party.

A delegate related the plans for a gay men's and lesbians' party that was to have taken place during the convention. The organizers were convinced to call it off following Wednesday night's party. This particular affair clearly had a political purpose behind it. For example, the comrade explained that as a supporter of the party's line on gay liberation, he was not invited, but that a comrade who isn't gay but opposes the majority's position on gay liberation was invited because he had a car and could get liquor for the party. It's utopian and naïve for comrades to think that political discussions do not happen at these kinds of exclusive gatherings. It's inherent in the character of such affairs that this will occur. Certain comrades are implicitly excluded on a political basis.

The logic of permitting these functions to occur could lead to a conception that there are questions of party policy that gays should discuss by themselves, that women should discuss by themselves, that Latinos should discuss by themselves, and that Blacks should discuss by themselves. It is true that in the mass movement, our comrades, when it is politically correct, participate in various caucuses—Black caucuses, women's caucuses, minority women's caucuses, etc., in order to help advance the struggle of especially oppressed sectors of the working class against the class-collaborationist domination of our class. And we defend the right of women, of Blacks, to have their own organizations, their own caucuses in the unions, on campus, etc.

But our conception of building the revolutionary party is totally different. We do not view the party as a coordinating committee of the leaderships of each sector of the mass movement. Our party is not composed of caucuses or caucus-like formations struggling for their "rights" in the party.

We are a centralized combat party and are attempting to forge a special type of instrument—the kind of organization that, as one delegate said, people are totally unaccustomed to when they join. Party members must have confidence and mutual trust in each other if they are going to go into battle together. And the democratically elected bodies of the party make all appropriate political decisions.

Here, I think the reference made by a comrade to Lenin's writings on the revolutionary party and the national question are well taken. Lenin's view was that we cannot allow the racism and hostility that exists toward the oppressed nationalities on the part of the oppressor nationality to be expressed in the party; nor can we allow the hostility that exists for the oppressor nationality by the oppressed nationalities to divide the party.

In a centralized multinational party, the place to organize discussion of political policy is in meetings of the appropriate bodies—executive committees, fractions, national and local conventions, National Committee, and so forth.

Another danger of exclusive functions is that they can breed cliquism. As a comrade put it, when you're left out of a gathering of comrades whom you like and want to socialize with because it excludes other people you want to be with, an atmosphere is created that you're not part of the "in group"—that you're not "nationalist" enough or "feminist" enough to be part of it. This is the breeding ground of cliquism.

I raise these points not because I think there is a big problem of polyvanguardism and cliquism in the party. Rather I wanted to summarize some of the very real political dangers to the party comrades have correctly pointed to with exclusive social events.

PARTY MEMBERSHIP AND ACTIVE SUPPORTERS

By Jack Barnes and Joel Britton

The first of the two items published below is an excerpt from an April 16, 1996, letter by Jack Barnes to the steering committee of the party's national fraction in the Union of Needletrades, Industrial and Textile Employees. UNITE resulted from the 1995 merger of the Amalgamated Clothing and Textile Workers Union and the International Ladies' Garments Workers' Union. The second item, written six years earlier, is a letter by Joel Britton to the party's branch executive committees.

Party recruitment and the turn to industry

[T]he Political Committee is convinced that the party's national trade union work has to begin being led by a body based among comrades in the field who have fraction steering committee experience and are ready to shoulder additional national leadership responsibility. We have to shed any illusion we can somehow lead our union work through a staff at the National Office or elsewhere. That's why we've urged the NTUC [National Trade Union Committee] to use its powers with fraction steering committees to take initiatives, even if this means taking on more "extra-trade-union" consultation with branch leaderships and Young Socialists chapters.

One of the questions the PC mandated the NTUC to discuss was helping to reverse the erosion we had begun to address during the NC conference in implementing the party's long-standing policies on recruitment, which are at the heart of *The Changing Face of U.S. Politics*. Specifically, the political report adopted by conference delegates reaffirmed the norm that recruitment to a turn party centers on winning industrial workers and others who agree to advance the party's work by becoming part of a union fraction and subordinating personal priorities to the weekly rhythm of branch activity.

The sole exception, explicitly discussed and decided by the party, is that branches can take in revolutionary-minded students whose activity and demonstrated commitment to the party's goals (including, since early 1994, as members of the Young Socialists) indicate they will join a branch jobs committee and get into a fraction after completing, as they see fit, their schooling. Just like workers or anyone else who comes around the communist movement, these young people are recruited *to a turn party*. They are admitted as party members, with no arm-twisting because of their temporary situation as students.

The success of the Minneapolis YS convention over the Easter weekend certainly confirms that, if we stick to this course, we can win a new layer of youth to the party and train them as worker-bolsheviks, wherever they come from.

In the political report to the NC leadership conference, we called attention to a recent example in the Boston branch where the party's recruitment policy had not been followed and the PC had rejected readmitting a former party member at this time. Several delegates reported that at least a few other branches had begun departing from this norm in recent years as well. So, in adopting the political reports and summaries to that gathering, we reaffirmed our criteria for recruitment to the party. The Political Committee asked the NTUC to have further discussion on this matter, and to pursue it each time they go to a branch or meet with a steering committee.

This policy is related to the broader question of party membership. We began discussing this, too, at the NC leadership conference, especially on the last day. The tendency of branches in recent years to turn inward politically has reinforced an inclination to go around branch structures and organize "branch activists"—rather than organizing the branch as a whole.

When I hear a comrade talk about how "we" participated in some political event, I find it's sometimes useful to think about whether the "we" being referred to is *the branch*. When we participate in a political activity or go out on a sale, of course, we do so with the comrades who've signed up, who've been assigned, or who turn out on Saturday or Sunday. That's the only way we can function. But we always lead by organizing the branch, through its weekly business meetings and committee structure, as well as through the fractions.

Getting that elementary norm of proletarian organization right is at the heart of putting the party in fighting trim to respond to struggles and political openings that come our way. It's central to strengthening the democracy and revolutionary centralist functioning of the party.

Only branches organized in this way can recruit workers who come around us through our fractions, plant-gate sales, or other political activity. That's what we're in business for—to recruit *workers* to a combat party and international communist movement. That's the top priority of every union fraction and party branch.

Moreover, only branches of this kind can collaborate with Young Socialists as part of a common movement and recruit the most committed of them to the party.

When we're retreating from organizing along these lines, then clarity about what constitutes party membership inevitably begins eroding too. Several things have called such slippage to our attention recently.

First, we began noticing around the time of the Cuba solidarity actions last October that it was becoming standard in some branches to invite active supporters and others to attend fraction meetings to prepare our participation in conferences, protests, and other activities.

Second, we've found that more branches seem to be taking in as active supporters co-workers who are involved in union and other political activity, and whose rhythm of life is the weekly rhythm of an industrial worker, but who we are not actively seeking to recruit as party members.

Third, we began noticing lists drawn up by branches with vague concentric circles of relations with the party—from members, to active supporters, to "other supporters" and finally "friends"!

In addition to blurring the rights and responsibilities of party members, such a "sliding scale" of comradeship also endangers a sustainable national formation of active supporters. Ever since we established active supporters as a category of membership in the communist movement, voted in by branch executive committees, we have emphasized that these individuals, "unlike members . . . do not subordinate personal priorities to those of the rhythm of a workers' party." [See the SWP's 1990 political resolution, "U.S. Imperialism Has Lost the Cold War," in *New International* no. 11.]

As such, active supporters are not members of our union fractions or branch committees (as opposed, in some cases, to committees organizing nonparty institutions such as bookstores or Militant Labor Forums), nor do they function as part of a disciplined party fraction in movements of social protest. They follow the *Militant* for political orientation, of course. And the party considers them politically accountable, as we do anyone else, for how they function in any political fight or organization they are involved in. But that is different from being under party discipline as part of our fraction in that organization or struggle.

Instead, active supporters are organized by the party to help advance our campaigns and propaganda institutions and to organize systematic financial support through monthly contributions to the national party treasury and systematic fundraising from others.

With these considerations in mind, co-workers or other industrial workers who become interested in the communist movement are generally people we should be working to recruit to the party, not vote in as active supporters. If they are sustaining the daily tempo of industrial work, are involved in the union, and are participating in political activity outside the workplace and union, then they should be capable of functioning as part of a centralized party of worker-bolsheviks.

Active supporters and national union fractions

14 Charles Lane
New York, NY 10014

February 15, 1990

TO BRANCH EXECUTIVE COMMITTEES

Dear Comrades,

The Political Committee recently reviewed the practice in a number of union fractions of having active supporters function as "members" of the fractions. Active supporters have been invited to attend entire fraction meetings with voice and "consultative" vote that in actual practice becomes more than consultative. These comrades also chair meetings, take minutes, give major reports, and take on other responsibilities of fraction members.

The Political Committee voted to reverse this course, which detracts from our goal of building a national active supporters formation and alters the character of our fractions as combat units of a communist party.

We are a workers' party. Many of our active supporters are workers and some of them work with us in industry. They, like other active supporters, can be a source of strength for the party in carrying out our campaigns when they are organized and led by the branch executive committee or another leadership body. Active supporters in industrial unions can be part of helping to carry out party political campaigns there as well.

Active supporters get their weekly political direction and lead from the *Militant*. Unlike members, active supporters do not attend branch meetings, which are a collective political experience that shapes our priorities and deepens our political clarity on a weekly basis.

When active supporters are incorporated into the weekly union fraction meetings as fraction "members," not everyone is there on an equal basis. Active supporters, not having been at the branch meeting, do not and cannot have the same framework of branch political and organizational priorities and other considerations in mind as the fraction works its way through its discussions and decisions. Such a meeting begins to take on more the character of a trade union group rather than a fraction of a communist party, despite the best of intentions and good will on the part of all concerned.

Having non-members of the party and YSA as fraction members detracts from the democratic norms we must maintain. Party and YSA members must be able to have the freest, frankest exchange of views in the fractions on how best to carry out our work in the unions. Having non-members present, many of whom are former branch leaders with strong opinions and abilities, cuts across this objective decision-making process among those who are responsible for this function and who, as party and YSA militants in worksites and union locals, will have to live with the results.

Working with active supporters in our unions is a challenge before any branch or district fraction and a variety of steps can be taken. We can delegate a fraction member or two to go over fraction decisions with the active supporters, which can often be an adequate form of collaboration. We can selectively invite these comrades to certain agenda points at some fraction meetings. However, any such invitations must be decided by the fraction as a whole. Our aim is to provide guidance, not impose on active supporters the discipline party militants assume as normal in our work.

Some of the active supporters who have come into the weekly rhythm of our work in their unions may want to consider joining or rejoining the party and assume full responsibilities for helping to construct the communist party necessary to the coming revolution. Most will not. We value whatever contribution anyone can make.

The party has growing opportunities to draw around it active supporters who agree to work with us and other active supporters to reach out and organize a broader layer of supporters, sympathizers, and friends of the party. Most recently, the political focus for this work has been the Pathfinder Mural Project.

The active supporters organize themselves as a group to aid the party on campaigns and to take responsibility for helping to obtain monthly sustaining pledges to help finance the party nationally among broader milieus. Where organized to do so, active supporters will also take responsibility for helping the party maintain and develop a long-term subscriber base for the *Militant*. Such support work can be developed only with the participation and leadership of active supporters, many of whom have substantial political experience. At the same time, we respect the decision active supporters have made not to be members who subordinate their lives to the rhythm and priorities of a turn party. We strive to insulate active supporters from all aspects of the internal life of the party. Any exceptions to this should be consciously and collectively decided upon by the appropriate party committees.

This policy of reorganizing our fractions on a local level along these lines will apply also to national industrial union fraction meetings. Specific decisions to invite an active supporter to a national fraction meeting can be made by an appropriate body.

Branch executive committees should organize a discussion on these matters in the branch and affected fractions. Please report in writing to the Organization and Trade Union Bureau on steps taken to implement this policy where a change in practice is required.

Comradely,

s/Joel Britton
for the Organization and
Trade Union Bureau

ALSO FROM PATHFINDER

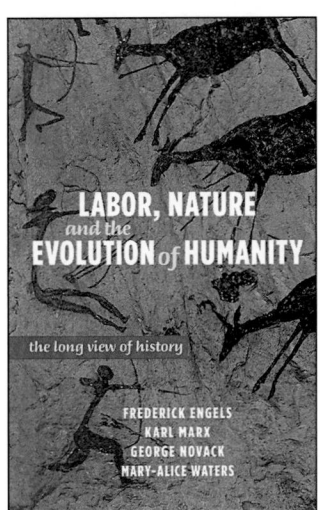

Labor, Nature, and the Evolution of Humanity
The Long View of History
FREDERICK ENGELS
KARL MARX
GEORGE NOVACK
MARY-ALICE WATERS

Without understanding that social labor, transforming nature, has driven humanity's evolution for millions of years, working people are unable to see beyond the capitalist epoch of class exploitation that warps all human relations, ideas, and values. Only the revolutionary conquest of state power by the working class can open the door to a world free of capitalist exploitation, degradation of nature, subjugation of women, racism, and war. A world built on human solidarity. A socialist world. $12. Also in Spanish and French.

The Teamster Series
FARRELL DOBBS

Four books on the 1930s strikes, organizing drives, and political campaigns that transformed the Teamsters into a militant industrial union movement. Written by the organizer of these battles and leader of the Socialist Workers Party.

A tool for workers seeking to use union power and advance the fight for a party of labor. $16 each, series $50. Also in Spanish. *Teamster Rebellion* is also available in French, Farsi, Greek.

The Clintons' Anti-Working-Class Record
Why Washington Fears Working People
JACK BARNES

What working people need to know about the profit-driven course of Democrats and Republicans alike over the last three decades. And the political awakening of workers seeking to understand and resist the capitalist rulers' assaults. $10. Also in Spanish, French, Farsi, Greek.

The Struggle for a Proletarian Party
JAMES P. CANNON

"The workers of America have power enough to topple the structure of capitalism at home and to lift the whole world with them when they rise," Cannon asserts. On the eve of World War II, a founder of the communist movement in the US and leader of the Communist International in Lenin's time defends the program and party-building norms of Bolshevism. $20. Also in Spanish and Farsi.

Is Socialist Revolution in the US Possible?
A Necessary Debate Among Working People
MARY-ALICE WATERS

An unhesitating "Yes"—that's the answer given here. Possible—but not inevitable. That depends on what working people *do*. $7. Also in Spanish, French, Farsi.

The Communist Manifesto
KARL MARX AND FREDERICK ENGELS

Communism, say the founding leaders of the revolutionary workers movement, is not a set of ideas or preconceived "principles" but workers' line of march to power. It springs from a "movement going on under our very eyes." $5. Also in Spanish, French, Farsi, Arabic.

PATHFINDERPRESS.COM

BUILDING A PROLETARIAN PARTY

In Defense of Marxism
Against the Petty-Bourgeois Opposition in the Socialist Workers Party
LEON TROTSKY

A reply to those in the revolutionary workers movement in the late 1930s who buckled to bourgeois patriotism during Washington's buildup to enter World War II. Trotsky explains why only a party fighting to bring workers into its ranks and leadership can steer a communist course. In the process, he defends the materialist and dialectical foundations of Marxism. $17. Also in Spanish, French, Farsi.

Cuba and the Coming American Revolution
JACK BARNES

This is a book about the example set by the Cuban people that socialist revolution is not only necessary—it can be made. A book about the struggles of workers and other exploited producers in the imperialist heartland, and the youth attracted to them. About the class struggle in the US, where the revolutionary capacities of working people are as utterly discounted by the ruling powers as were those of the Cuban toilers. $10. Also in Spanish, French, Farsi.

Revolutionary Continuity
Marxist Leadership in the U.S.
The Early Years, 1848–1917
Birth of the Communist Movement, 1918–1922
FARRELL DOBBS

"Successive generations of proletarian revolutionists have participated in the movements of the working class and its allies. . . . Marxists today owe them not only homage for their deeds. We also have a duty to learn what they did wrong as well as right so their errors are not repeated." —*Farrell Dobbs.* Two volumes, $17 each.

The Transitional Program for Socialist Revolution
LEON TROTSKY

The Socialist Workers Party program, drafted by Bolshevik leader Trotsky in 1938, still guides communists the world over. The party "uncompromisingly gives battle to all political groupings tied to the apron strings of the bourgeoisie. Its task—the abolition of capitalism's domination. Its aim—socialism. Its method—the proletarian revolution." $17. Also in Farsi.

Counter-Mobilization
A Strategy to Fight Racist and Fascist Attacks
FARRELL DOBBS

A discussion on strategy and tactics in the fight against fascist attacks on the labor movement, drawing on the experiences of the Minneapolis Teamsters movement of the 1930s. $5

Their Trotsky and Ours
JACK BARNES

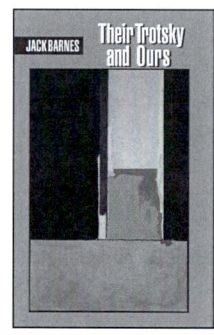

To lead the working class in a successful revolution, a mass proletarian party is needed whose cadres, well beforehand, have absorbed a world communist program, are proletarian in life and work, derive deep satisfaction from doing politics, and have forged a leadership with an acute sense of what to do next. This book is about building such a party. $12. Also in Spanish, French, Farsi.

Lenin's Final Fight
Speeches and Writings, 1922–23
V.I. LENIN

In 1922 and 1923, V.I. Lenin, central leader of the world's first socialist revolution, waged what was to be his last political battle—one that was lost after his death. At stake was whether that revolutionary government and the world communist movement it led would remain on the revolutionary proletarian course that brought workers and peasants to power in Russia in 1917. $17. Also in Spanish, Farsi, Greek.

DEFENDING WORKERS' RIGHTS

Socialism on Trial
TESTIMONY AT MINNEAPOLIS SEDITION TRIAL
James P. Cannon

The revolutionary program of the working class presented in federal court in 1941 on the eve of US entry into World War II. The frame-up charges of "seditious conspiracy" targeted leaders of the Socialist Workers Party. $15. Also in Spanish, French, Farsi.

Cointelpro
THE FBI'S SECRET WAR ON POLITICAL FREEDOM
Nelson Blackstock

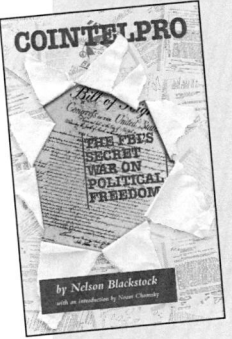

An in-depth look at the 1960s and '70s covert FBI disruption and counterintelligence program—code-named COINTELPRO. Contains reproductions of FBI documents released through the Socialist Workers Party suit against government spying. $15

50 Years of Covert Operations in the US
WASHINGTON'S POLITICAL POLICE AND THE AMERICAN WORKING CLASS
Larry Seigle, Farrell Dobbs, Steve Clark

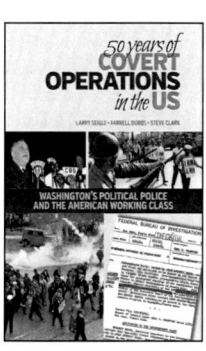

How class-conscious workers have defended constitutional freedoms and fought the capitalists' drive to build the "national security" state essential to maintaining their rule. $10. Also in Spanish and Farsi.

FBI on Trial
THE VICTORY IN THE SOCIALIST WORKERS PARTY SUIT AGAINST GOVERNMENT SPYING
Margaret Jayko

The record of a historic victory in the fight for political rights, including the 1986 federal court ruling against government spying and excerpts from trial testimony by SWP leaders Farrell Dobbs and Jack Barnes. $17

PATHFINDERPRESS.COM

EXPAND YOUR REVOLUTIONARY LIBRARY

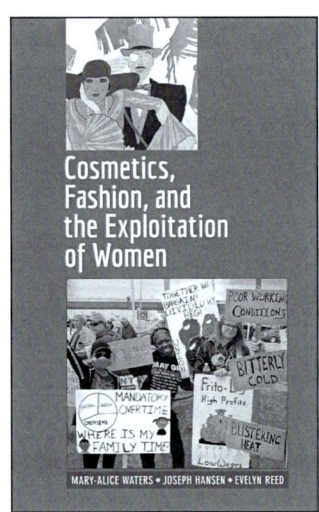

New Edition!
Cosmetics, Fashion, and the Exploitation of Women
MARY-ALICE WATERS
JOSEPH HANSEN
EVELYN REED

"Norms of beauty and fashion are inseparable from the class struggle." That's the title of the opening chapter of this timely new edition of a lively 1950s debate in the *Militant*, a socialist newsweekly. How cosmetics and fashion monopolies rake in profits from social insecurities of women and adolescents. Why women's integration into the workforce and unions is a major advance in the fight for emancipation. A Marxist classic on the origins of women's oppression and the working-class road forward. $15. Also in Spanish, French, Farsi, Greek.

New!
Revolution and the Road to Peace in Colombia
The Example of the Cuban Revolution
FIDEL CASTRO

"No crime can be committed in the name of revolution," Fidel Castro declares, drawing from the example set by working people of Cuba as they took state power out of the hands of its capitalist rulers. In 2008, as part of efforts to end six decades of armed conflict in Colombia, he shared the exemplary record of Cuba's revolutionary struggle with the Revolutionary Armed Forces of Colombia (FARC) and the world. $10. Also in Spanish and French.

Imperialism's March Toward Fascism and War
JACK BARNES

"There will be new Hitlers, new Mussolinis. That is inevitable. What is not inevitable is that they will triumph. The working-class vanguard will organize our class to fight back against the devastating toll we are made to pay for the capitalist crisis. The future of humanity will be decided in the contest between these contending class forces." In *New International* no. 10. $14. Also in Spanish, French, Farsi, Greek.

Women in Cuba: The Making of a Revolution Within the Revolution
VILMA ESPÍN, ASELA DE LOS SANTOS
YOLANDA FERRER

The integration of women in the ranks and leadership of the Cuban Revolution was intertwined with the proletarian course led by Fidel Castro from the start. This is the story of that revolution and how it transformed the women and men who made it. $17. Also in Spanish, Farsi, Greek.

Labor's Giant Step
The First Twenty Years of the CIO: 1936–55
ART PREIS

The story of the explosive labor struggles and political battles in the 1930s that built the industrial unions. And how those unions became the vanguard of a mass social movement that began transforming US society. $27

Pathfinder Press accessible e-books for the blind, those with low vision, or other challenges reading print books

For a list of current accessible titles, go to: pathfinderpress.com/collections/books-for-the-blind.

Visit bookshare.org for information on how to sign up.